The Mythology of North America ↘

John Bierhorst

THE MYTHOLOGY OF NORTH AMERICA

William Morrow and Company

NEW YORK·

Library of Congress Cataloging in Publication Data

Bierhorst, John/The mythology of North America

Bibliography/p.
Summary/Describes the background of the myths of the Indian
cultures of the North American continent, some of which have
the same themes as myths of other world cultures.
1. Indians of North America—Religion and mythology.
[1. Indians of North America—Religion and mythology] I. Title.
E98.R3B54 1985   291.1'3'08997   85-281
ISBN 0-688-04145-0

Sources for pictures on pp. 9, 11, 33, 43, 87–89, 162–63, and
175–77 are Hall, Blackman, and Rickard; Wheelwright; Barbeau 1950;
Barbeau 1950; Reichard 1939; Catlin 1976; and Dorsey 1905a, respectively.
For full authors' names, titles, and publication data, see the bibliographies
in the back of this book. Photographs on pp. 31, 51 (upper), and
51 (lower) are courtesy of National Museums of Canada, negatives
70399, 87389, and 87390. All other credits are given in the
captions that accompany the illustrations. Every effort has been
made to contact copyright owners. Where older material has
been reproduced, or if the present whereabouts of
artists or collectors could not be determined, credit has been
given to the fullest extent possible.

*Frontispiece/*thunderbird (F. Newcomb and G. Reichard, *Sandpaintings of
the Navajo Shooting Chant,* New York, 1975.)

Contents ↰

v ·

48736

Illustrations ↶

vii ·

Maps ⤹

A Note on Pronunciation

Names of mythological persons and certain other words from Indian languages have been printed in italics to indicate that they may be pronounced according to a simplified system. The rules are that consonants and consonant combinations have their usual English values; vowels are as in Spanish or Italian *(a = ah, e = eh, i = ee, o = oh, u = oo);* and the accent mark, if present, shows which syllable should receive the main stress. Such a system rides roughshod over the subtleties of accurate pronunciation but may at least prevent some of the worst mishaps.

Introduction ✎

Past and present

Mythology does not have the antiquity of geologic ages, but it is nevertheless a very old pattern, woven into the terrain over the course of thousands of years. Each continent—except Antarctica —has its own mythological imprint and will probably never receive another, at least not in the foreseeable future. Myths are not sown like gardens; they are inherited from the past. Viewed at a distance, myths create a luxuriant configuration that gradually changes from region to region. At close range, these same myths reflect the desires and fears of distinct peoples, granting them trusteeship of the land with the consent of unseen powers.

At what point the North American pattern became fixed in its present form we have no way of knowing. It can be said with some assurance that the myths of eastern Canada, still alive in oral tradition, have not changed in three hundred and fifty years. Archaeological remains do not preserve myths, but the apparent continuity of town-dwelling cultures in the eastern Southwest implies that the sacred stories of that area could be a thousand years old. They, too, are still alive.

Mythological traditions hang by a thread in the states of New York and Washington and have been broken off completely in Georgia and Virginia. In New York, for example, the Iroquois still tell some of their old stories, but in Virginia there are no living traces of Indian culture. The continental pattern emerges, however, in the mass of stories told for the record by Indian mythmakers since the arrival of the first Europeans.

The floodgates of narration opened widest during the time when Indian mythology was at its most vulnerable. This was the roughly fifty-year period between the General Allotment Act of 1887 and the Indian Reorganization Act of 1934. Both were acts of the United States Congress, the first a means of dissolving Indian communities, the second a step toward reestablishing them when for many it was too late.

During the years between, Indian traditionalists persuaded themselves to share their myths in exchange for the promise that their words would be preserved in books. In this at least they were not deceived.

Today the erosion of live myth continues at a rapid pace. At the same time, there are signs that the loss may have slowed somewhat. In the early 1900s, at the lowest ebb of Indian vitality, when it became fashionable to speak of the "vanishing race," few would have believed that Indian mythology, still functional, could have made its way into the twenty-first century. Aided by a changed political climate, it is about to do just that.

The first century and a half

Although Jesuit missionaries had collected a few myths east of the Great Lakes in the 1600s, the modern appreciation of Indian myth and the idea of recording entire mythologies originated with the explorer and Indian agent Henry Rowe Schoolcraft, whose diary entry for July 31, 1822, expresses his elation at having stumbled on something new: "Who would have imagined that these wandering foresters should have possessed such a resource? What have all the voyagers and remarkers from the days of Cabot and Raleigh been about, not to have discovered this curious trait, which lifts up indeed a curtain, as it were, upon the Indian mind, and exhibits it in an entirely new character?"

Schoolcraft echoes the European romantics who were already cultivating homegrown alternatives to Greek and Latin lore. In some respects his two volumes of Chippewa tales, published in 1839 under the title *Algic Researches,* stand as an American counterpart to Jacob and Wilhelm Grimm's two-volume *Kinder- und Hausmärchen,* or *Fairy Tales* (1812–15). Like the Brothers Grimm, Schoolcraft would be recognized by later generations as a pioneer and, again like the Grimms, would be accused of rewriting his sources.

At the turn of the century, when Franz Boas and his co-workers began building a science of anthropology in the United States, it became apparent that myths and folktales would play a major role. This was partly because myths were texts that could be used in the decipherment of Indian languages, and partly because they were often the only remnant of cultures that had ceased to exist.

As the newly collected mythologies of the Navajo, the Hopi, the Coos, the Caddo, the Kwakiutl, and other tribes rolled off scholarly presses, Boas took the lead in describing the basic tale types and motifs—or plots and incidents—observing that "myths have traveled from tribe to tribe, and that a large body of legends belongs to many in common." One reason for this approach was that myths helped establish historical connections between tribes that had separated, offering clues to the development of native American societies.

The grand exercise in "typing" and "motifing" was carried out not by an anthropologist but by the folklorist Stith Thompson, whose annotated *Tales of the North American Indians* (1929) drew heavily on the work of Boas and his school. By this time Boas had finished his distributional studies and, with other anthropologists, had begun to view myth primarily as a key to unlocking the secrets of a single culture. A turning point came with the publication in 1935 of Ruth Benedict's *Zuni Mythology,* embracing all the tales that had been recorded from Zuni pueblo over the previous fifty years. "No folktale is generic," she declared in her introductory essay. "It is always the tale of one particular people with one particular livelihood and social organization and religion."

A generation later, Benedict's particularity no longer seemed narrow enough to some, who were now increasingly aware of the differences between storytellers. In the 1950s the approach to anthropology known as "culture and personality," which Benedict had helped to establish, shifted emphasis from the "personality" of the whole culture to the personality of the individual within the culture. Collectors of Indian myths began to have as much to say about their informants as about the myths they told, showing how the sex, age, or psychology of the teller affected the story. Carried forward by a general interest in feminism, the trend continued into the 1980s with studies of women storytellers and of attitudes toward women as revealed in myth.

Meanwhile, beginning in the 1960s, another group of myth collectors focused even more narrowly, capturing not the personality of the storyteller but merely his storytelling performance. This was accomplished by printing translations that showed where the narrator paused to catch his breath, where he changed his tone of voice, and what sounds or comments his audience made. With precision like this, ethnographers had come a long way from Schoolcraft, whose literary efforts had been questioned even before the era of Boas' great influence.

By concentrating on the narrator's art rather than on his personal traits, the performance ethnographers dignified the Indian storyteller in a way that had never been done before and so made a timely, if subtle, political statement. In line with this development, native groups began to publish their own myths and traditional narratives, primarily for the sake of their children. Two of the earliest and most noteworthy collections were the Rough Rock Demonstration School's *Navajo History,* vol. 1 (1971) and *The Zunis: Self-Portrayals* (1972), which carries the byline "the Zuni people."

Through all these changes, myths have continued to accumulate. The total has more than doubled since 1920, the date arbitrarily fixed by Margaret Mead and Ruth Bunzel as marking the end of the "golden age" in American anthropology. Today probably no one could claim, as Stith Thompson once did, that he had read every Indian tale in print. On the other hand, numerous regional studies of North American myth have increased the possibility of viewing it as a whole, and since no systematic description has appeared in nearly seventy years (H. B. Alexander's *North American Mythology* was published in 1916), it would seem that the time had come to make a fresh attempt.

"As if a man walked"

This is a book about mythology—the important tales—not about folktales in general, which would include stories of romance, adventure tales, and humorous anecdotes. Nevertheless, it is difficult to separate myths from other kinds of narrative, and it is certainly true that mythology owes its existence to storytelling. In the case of a clan or a religious society, the sharing of a myth may actually hold the group together. Sometimes an ordinary folktale that has passed from one language to another will be recognized as a myth by the people who have received it and will be used to explain the origin of a tribe, a religious ceremony, or a source of food. Such stories are always believed to be old.

In North America, where more than a hundred native languages are still spoken and oral traditions once passed freely between cultures, storytellers have tended to divide narratives into two basic categories. Typically, the Eskimo used to speak of old stories and young stories. Among the Winnebago, stories were either *waikan* (sacred) or simply *worak* (narrated). To the

Pawnee, the distinction was between true and false. The second of the two categories, which varies from tribe to tribe, can refer to fiction, nonfiction, or a mixture of both; mainly it sets up a contrast with the first category, which, whether defined as old, sacred, or true, corresponds to the English word "myth."

Myths and ordinary tales alike were widely regarded as persons. In the Northeast a storyteller might begin by announcing, "It is as if a man walked," or "Here lives my story," or "Here camps my story," or even, "My story was walking along, a wilderness house man, his clothing was made of sheets of moss, and shreds of withes formed his belt." This implies that the story is ancient. When finished, a California narrator might order his story to go back to its cave. Or, if in the mood for an additional tale, an Eskimo teller would say to his audience, "You can't leave it standing on one leg."

More often the opening announcement would amount to nothing but a simple "Long ago," to which the audience would respond, "It is so." But even where not regarded as persons, stories had to be treated with respect. Among the Tlingit, children who fidgeted would have their feet tied together. Sometimes preliminary prayers were necessary. If an important myth was being told, experts in the audience might correct the narrator while in progress. And in nearly every tribe it was considered dangerous to tell stories except at particular times.

When James Mooney published his collection of Cherokee myths in 1900, he felt the need to comment on his discovery that the Cherokee told stories all year round, day or night. Although the study of Indian lore was still a young science, enough information had accumulated to suggest what would soon be recognized as a continent-wide rule: stories, or at least some stories, could be told only at night and only during the winter. From tribe to tribe the reasons given were similar. According to the Coast Salish of Washington, snakes would crawl through the door if stories were heard in summer. According to the Wyandot, the snakes would crawl into your bed. They would choke you, added the Seneca, and bees would sting your lips.

Presumably because the oldness of myths, like a disease, might be contagious, Coast Salish storytellers and their listeners had to lie flat on the ground to keep from getting a hump between the shoulders. The same old-age deformity can be brought on by summer storytelling, according to the Zuni, and in California it was once said that even to think about stories during the day would give one a humpback.

Gathered around winter fires, protected by prayers and precautions, North Americans shared the old stories, reshaped them, and built a vast pattern of interrelated mythologies. As the stories gradually change from tribe to tribe, the pattern itself changes, especially from south to north. At the same time it displays a remarkable unity, west to east, over distances ranging from two thousand miles in the south to four thousand miles in the far north.

The oldest stories

The earliest reliably dated archaeological finds in the New World are of hunting implements abandoned at woolly mammoth and long-horned bison kill sites between ten thousand and fifteen thousand years ago, long after the disappearance of pre-modern man but before the advent of either agriculture or ocean travel. From this follows the theory that the first Americans were hunters, who arrived by way of the only link between the hemispheres, the Siberia-Alaska land bridge, which remained above water until about 8000 B.C. More recent arrivals, including the Athapascans and the Eskimo, no doubt took the same route, crossing on winter ice.

Unquestionably these migrants brought with them the skills to make weapons, fur clothing, and shelters against the cold. It seems safe to assume that they also brought a store of intellectual culture, which would have included myths and perhaps even folktales. But which myths? And which folktales?

Among myths, the most impressive candidate for Old World origin has been the famous Earth Diver, the story of water creatures who take turns diving for a piece of solid land. The duck,

the muskrat, the turtle, the crawfish, or some other animal succeeds but has had to dive so deep that by the time he returns he
is half drowned or dead. In his claws, however, the others find a
bit of mud that they magically enlarge until it becomes the earth.
Not every Indian tribe has a myth about the creation of the earth.
But of those that do, most have this one. It is found in all regions
of North America except the Southwest and the arctic coasts.

The more or less continuous distribution of The Earth Diver
from Europe through Asia to Alaska and southward argues per-
suasively for a historical connection. Even more widespread than
The Earth Diver is the mythic concept of the world flood. It turns
up in most mythologies, either as primeval water or as a deluge
brought about by accident. Since the idea is embedded in many
different myths (including The Earth Diver), it must be regarded
as a motif, not a story, and the theory that it has been continually
reinvented would be hard to refute.

Less common, but also of world distribution, is The Theft of
Fire, in which a creature sets out to steal fire from a distant
source, obtains it, often through trickery, and carries it home.
The best-known version is the Greek myth of Prometheus. But
the story also occurs in the southeastern United States and in the
region west of the Rockies. In Canada and Alaska it is sometimes
replaced by the similar Theft of the Sun or Theft of Daylight, or
even Theft of Heat.

In the realm of folktales, several items of far-flung distribution
have been noticed repeatedly, among them the so-called Orpheus tale. In its simplest form this story tells of a husband who
journeys westward in search of his wife, who has become a ghost.
After finding her in the land of the dead, he receives permission
to take her home, but with the warning that he will lose her
forever if he touches her during the return trip, looks at her, or
breaks a similar prohibition. On the way back he does break the

---

The Theft of the Sun. Raven (*at right*) is shown releasing the sun, which
he has carried to earth in a wooden box. Silk-screen print, 1978, by
Calvin Hunt, Kwakiutl.

prohibition, and according to some storytellers this accounts for the origin of permanent death. The tale is characteristic of North America, occurring in all regions except the far north. Probably because it recalls the Greek myth of Orpheus and Eurydice, the attempt has been made to trace it through Asia to the Bering Strait. The results, however, are inconclusive.

Another of the relatively few folktales distributed across the continent is The Bird Nester, regarded by some tribes as a major myth. Typically, it tells of a father and a son and of the father's stratagem to win the woman they both desire. To get rid of the son, the father induces him to climb to a high nest, from which he is unable to return. Rescued finally by a supernatural helper, the son takes revenge on the father, who in the meantime has taken the woman.

Since The Bird Nester occurs also in South America, it has presumably been circulating in the New World for a long time, though no one has yet tried to show that it originated in Asia. The point to be made is that there is evidently an ancient stratum in North American mythology, represented by stories like The Earth Diver, The Theft of Fire, the Orpheus tale, and The Bird Nester. Considering its continental expanse and its prominence among tribes that continued to emphasize hunting and the gathering of wild plants, it may well predate the development of agriculture, which goes back more than five thousand years in North America.

Significantly, all the stories described up to this point have variants in which the actors are animals. In The Earth Diver and The Theft of Fire there is sometimes no principal actor, rather a council of animals, occasionally arguing but usually helping one another or taking turns. More often one animal dominates, becoming the protagonist in a series of stories, known to folklo-

---

The Theft of Fire. A sand painting of the Navajo Blessingway, showing Coyote bringing fire from the Fire God (*lower left*) to the hearth of First Man and First Woman (*upper left*). Courtesy of the Wheelwright Museum of the American Indian, Santa Fe.

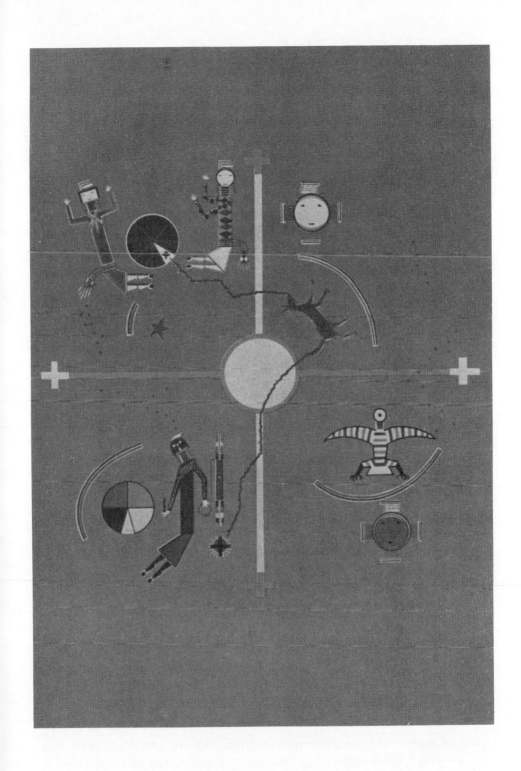

rists as a "cycle." Any group of stories on a single theme may be called by this name. But it is most commonly applied to the seemingly endless tales of animal or animal-like characters. Typical examples are the Hare and Rabbit cycles of the Midwest and East, and the Spider, Coyote, and Raven cycles of the West.

The trickster

According to an Apache storyteller, Coyote wore clothes in the stories but walked on all fours and had the body of a coyote. Another storyteller from the same tribe expressed a different opinion: "I think of him as being just like a man when I tell about him, with face, hands, and feet like a man. They say that all the animals were people in those days."

Either way, the creature is in some sense a person, as are all animal protagonists in world folklore. For many Indian tribes this ambiguous condition defines the so-called myth age, which is widely regarded as an age of animals. Usually, the myth age ends when the "people" are changed into the animals of today.

Romantic folktales in which a human heroine or hero passes into the animal world, often as a bride or bridegroom, dramatize the importance of animals, especially as sources of food. Pueblo Deer Boy, Plains Buffalo Wife, and the widespread Bear Maiden and Bear Mother stories typically include hunting themes and in many cases are treated as full-fledged myths.

When the protagonist is an animal, however, the term "hero" cannot be used as easily. It should be kept in mind that animals are considered dangerous or at least unpredictable. When they appear as mythic characters, they seldom prove altruistic. In the most popular tales they are tricksters, ranging from the playful to the outrageous.

At their worst, Indian tricksters pose as baby-sitters and eat the babies, or they disguise themselves as women in order to marry men. In one of the best-known stories of the western hemisphere, told from California to the Great Lakes and south as far as Tierra del Fuego, the trickster falls in love with his own daughter and pretends to die, advising the young woman that as soon as he is dead she will meet a stranger whom she must not fail to take as her husband. After digging out of his grave, or rolling off his funeral pyre, the trickster reappears in a disguise and marries the daughter. If he has two daughters, he marries them both.

Tales like this would seem suitable for the men's lodge, where in fact they were often told. But Robert Lowie, the Crow ethnographer, believed that women of the old school were probably no more prudish than men, and Melville Jacobs made a point of congratulating his Coos informant, a woman, who "has held out with a sense of humor against the new taboos."

Modern observers conditioned by Christianity may wish to believe that Indian mythologies are as chaste and as sober as their own—as indeed they are in some cases. But it must be remembered that violence, sexuality, and even irreverent comedy are essential to many ancient traditions, including those of Greece and Rome. In North America these elements are most noticeable in the trickster cycles found north of the Colorado River and west of the Great Lakes. To ignore them would be to miss an important aspect of the sacred lore of that part of the continent.

In many stories the trickster himself is the one tricked. For example, in the familiar Eye-Juggler tale the trickster imitates birds who toss their eyes in the air; but unlike the birds the trickster cannot restore his eyesight when the game is over. In another tale, The Bungling Host, he is entertained at the home of a friend, who provides dinner by slicing meat from his own flanks, which magically heal, or by butchering his own child, who returns to life. When the trickster himself plays host, in imitation of his friend, the trick fails to work and he ends up with lacerated flanks or a permanently dead child.

Can such stories be truly regarded as myths? For the Zuni, the Iroquois, and the Pawnee the answer is no. But both the Navajo and the Chippewa have included The Bungling Host and other trickster tales among their sacred traditions. For the nineteenth-century Omaha, The Bungling Host was evidently a myth about the origin of food, in which the trickster on different occasions is served a beaver's child, rice magically produced from water, nuts from a squirrel, and fish from a kingfisher.

The Theft of Fire is the classic example of a myth that is also a trickster tale. The Earth Diver falls into the same category if, as in the Yuchi variants, the mud at the bottom of the water is said to be stolen from the fish who owns it. In a Tanana version, Raven kidnaps the fish mother's child, refusing to give it back until she has brought up enough mud and gravel to build the Alaskan peninsula.

Since the trickster's antics have a way of leading to acts of creation, he is susceptible of being treated as a god, even if he has the personality of a devil. As if to clarify the situation, some tribal mythologies distinguish between two kinds of Coyote, or two kinds of Spider. The Cheyenne used to do this by relegating tales of low comedy and violence to *Wihio* (spider or wise one), whereas creation stories were told of *Heammawihio* (wise one above). In other tribes there is a tendency to give the trickster a companion, so that we have stories about Coyote and Skunk, Coyote and Wolf, or Coyote and Fox. In some cases, the two personalities recall the modern distinction between good and evil.

Throughout, there is a persistent tendency to deemphasize the trickster's animal nature. Although the Sioux trickster *Inktomi* (spider) is supposed to be a small man in tight brown leggings, it is doubtful that many Sioux have considered him a spider as such. The Cheyenne *Wihio* is even less spiderlike. When it comes to the Winnebago *Wakjunkaga,* no no one knows the origin of his name and he is never spoken of as other than human.

Gods and heroes

The trickster is most at home in the mythologies of the hunter-gatherer cultures. In the agricultural societies he slips to a secondary role, giving way to the anthropomorphic figures that many writers have called gods. Thus we hear of the Zuni war gods, the dying god of the Yumans, and the high gods of the Pawnee. The Zuni and the Pawnee relegate the trickster to the category of light literature, whereas the Yumans, like the Navajo, include him in myths as a lesser character.

The highest of the deities are remote originators who give the creation story its start, then often disappear. These have been reported sporadically from nearly all regions and reach their fullest development in north central California. In parts of the Southwest the originators are Mother Earth and Father Sky. A Wichita creation myth collected at the turn of the century opens with a fleeting glimpse of *Kinnekasus* (man never known on earth). A personage called Old One plays a similar part in certain Plateau stories. In at least a few cases there is a suspicion of Christian influence.

Ordinarily a tribe's mythology focuses on a character who inhabits the earth throughout the myth age, preparing it for the day-to-day needs of humans. Such a figure is called a culture hero. As creator and provider he may set the sun in its course, establish dry land, make rivers, create humans, release impounded game animals, and teach ceremonies. Or he may be a deliverer, who rids the world of man-eating monsters. If so, the stories about him are called a monster-ridding cycle.

"Transformer" is another term widely applied to the culture hero, whether he is a provider or a deliverer. Strictly speaking, it refers to the kind of hero who does not create or release the food supply but transforms myth-age "people" into game animals; and rather than killing monsters, he reduces their size or changes them into stones. The classic transformer cycles belong to the Northwest Coast and Plateau regions.

Most culture heroes, including transformers, combine the attributes of the provider and the deliverer, and in some tribes the culture hero is actually the trickster. No one has made a systematic effort to label these hybrids, but terms like "trickster-transformer" and "trickster-creator-transformer" have often been used.

One rule that holds almost everywhere is that the trickster is male. In Crow mythology, Coyote has a wife, who teaches the female arts of tanning hides and preparing pemmican, but she is not a trickster. Spider Woman (no relation to the trickster Spider) turns up as a helpful grandmother in a great many myths west of the Mississippi. At times she is dangerous, but she is never a buffoon.

By and large, the important female figures in American mythology, unless they can be said to represent plants or the earth, are fully anthopomorphic. Outstanding examples are Changing Woman, the earth goddess of the Navajo; Sedna, the Eskimo mistress of sea animals; Mother Corn of the Arikara; and the Shawnee creator, Our Grandmother. Generally speaking, these figures are providers. But in the Great Basin myth of People Mother, we have a female deliverer. Mother Corn is also a deliverer in that she leads the animal people out of the earth, a role played by the male war gods in Zuni myth.

It has been mentioned that the trickster is sometimes given a companion. Likewise, gods and heroes have companions or even twins. The Iroquois creators are twins, Changing Woman is paired with White Shell Woman, and the dying god of the Yumans usually has a twin. The list could be extended indefinitely. In many cases the two have unequal personalities, implying abstract pairs such as wise and foolish, senior and junior, and strong and weak, as well as good and evil.

Mythological regions

Despite a universal insistence on the antiquity of myths, including native testimony to the effect that myths must not vary, experience suggests that every narrator creates his or her own version. The idea that these versions flow together into units we can call Pawnee, Cree, or Pomo mythology requires that obvious differences be brushed aside. If we try to combine such units into larger groups based on language, location, or culture, the loss of detail becomes still more troublesome.

Language helps little. It can be shown, for example, that the neighboring Yurok, Karok, and Hupa of northwestern California shared a single body of myth, while speaking totally unrelated languages. Both the Hupa and the distant Navajo speak Athapascan languages, yet their mythologies have nothing significant in common. Evidently location helps more than language.

In fact, anthropologists in the United States have for years used location as a means of organizing almost any American Indian topic. The trend began in the 1890s, partly in reaction to evolutionary schemes that grouped cultures by how primitive or advanced they seemed. Accordingly, North America has been divided into about ten areas, the number depending on whose system is being followed. The Smithsonian's twenty-volume *Handbook of North American Indians,* which began publication in 1978, recognizes these: Arctic, Subarctic, Northwest Coast, California, Southwest, Great Basin, Plateau, Plains, Southeast, and Northeast. Earlier systems tended to define the last three differently, recognizing Plains, Prairie, and East. Each area is felt to have its own style or styles of culture.

But mythology, like music, art, housing, diet, or any other single aspect of culture, creates a pattern of its own, even if it conforms to generalized culture areas in certain respects. When the musicologist George Herzog began his continent-wide analysis of Indian song in the 1920s, he attempted to describe what came to be known as "musical areas." Mythological areas have never been seriously proposed, but if a subject as complex as North American myth is to be described with minimum loss of detail, it will be helpful to have them.

The accompanying map shows how they might look, though it is offered as no more than a tentative scheme for organizing this book. Avoiding novelty as much as possible, it closely follows the traditional culture areas, except that the Midwest (or Prairie region) has been shifted eastward, the southern part of the Northwest Coast has been joined with the Plateau to create a Coast-Plateau region, southern California has been included in the Southwest, and the eastern half of the Subarctic has been divided between the Midwest and the Northeast. The eleven regions, with their main features, are as follows:

Northwest Coast: trickster, transformer, clan and lineage myths
Arctic, or Eskimo: mistress of sea animals (east), trickster (west), songs in myths
Subarctic Athapascan: transformer, trickster
Southwest: emergence myth, monster-ridding cycle, dying god (Yuman type), migration legends, songs in myths

California: transformer, originator myths, animal myths, trickster
Great Basin: trickster, dying god (Basin type), heroine myths
Coast-Plateau: transformer, trickster
Plains: hero tales, trickster
Southeast: hero tales, trickster, council of animals
Northeast: culture-hero cycle
Midwest: trickster, dying god (Midwest type), clan myths

Such an arrangement implies a folkloristic view of mythology, emphasizing the distribution of themes and myth types. But it is no more than a framework within which to consider how myths both reflect and influence the lives of the people who use them.

Myth and culture

It has already been suggested that there may be mythological differences between the hunter-gatherers and the agriculturists. Buffalo Wife and Mother Corn myths make obvious references to the two kinds of economy. But why do hunter-gatherers favor trickster cycles, and why do farmers tell stories in which the first people emerge from the earth? Many writers feel certain that emergence myths symbolize pregnancy and delivery, which in turn symbolize the crop yield. Observations like this, however, are seldom supported by native testimony. As for the trickster, it has been theorized that he stands for the shaman, the unpredictable religious specialist in hunter societies, often feared as a witch.

Whether or not trickster tales satirize the shaman, there are obvious connections between mythology and religion. Although American Indian religious ceremonies never dramatize a story in the modern sense and often involve spirits not mentioned in myth, they do make reference to mythic characters and mythic events. Even Coyote is the subject of a nine-day ceremony of the Navajo. Conversely, ceremonial spirits like the Faces of the Iroquois or the Big Head of central California work their way into myth and become at least minor characters.

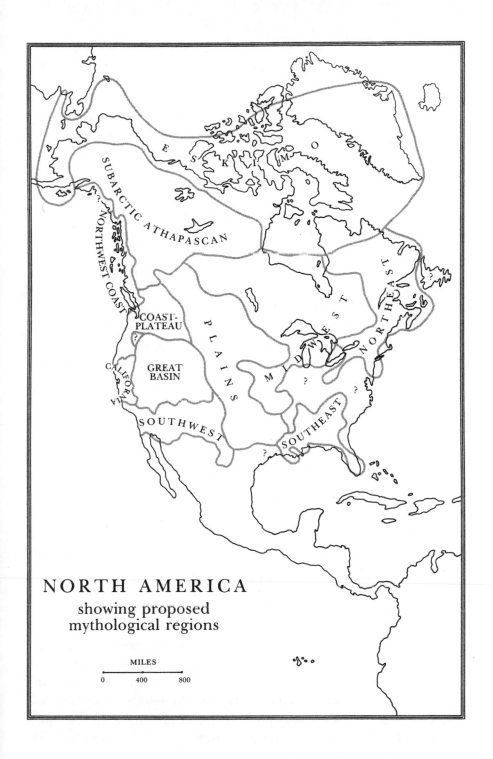

NORTH AMERICA

showing proposed
mythological regions

MILES

0   400   800

In addition, myths and folktales are used to explain how ceremonies come into existence. For example, a Navajo variant of
The Bird Nester tells how the hero learned the Bead Chant from
the supernaturals who rescued him from the nest. Stories of this
type prompted the anthropologist Bronislaw Malinowski to
define myth in general as "a warrant, a charter, and often even
a practical guide to the activities with which it is concerned."
Stories that fully deserve to be called charter myths, in the Mali-
nowskian sense, are often so crammed with descriptions of ceremonial rules and procedures that they become more charter than
story.

Mythology accounts for the origins and privileges of clans,
especially in the Midwest and along the Northwest Coast. Clan
myths, too, are charter myths.

For many tribes, notably in the Southwest, myth becomes history, accounting for the origin of a particular ethnic group, sometimes blending with a tale of tribal wanderings that may include
historically verifiable events. Such stories have been called legends. Also legendary are the stories of a hero or heroine who
gives a tribe new vitality during a period of stress. These are rare
and sometimes hard to identify. Sweet Medicine of the Cheyenne,
the Iroquois *Deganawida,* and the Sioux White Buffalo Calf
Woman are probably the best examples.

Mythology gives expression to the oldest of the sciences, as-
tronomy. Numerous myths account for the origin of the solar year
and of constellations, especially the Pleiades. In general, Indian
myths assume a three-level universe, consisting of sky, earth surface, and underworld.

Mythology reflects the art of the singer and of the orator,
producing distinctive styles. Examples will be found in the following pages.

Finally, mythology provides themes for painters and sculptors.
Just as ritualists do not dramatize myths, traditional Indian artists
do not illustrate them scene by scene, except in isolated cases.
Usually, only one character will be represented, or the artist will
create a symbolic composition for the entire story. Navajo sand
painting and Northwest Coast carving have probably gained the

greatest fame. Examples of these and other native American art traditions—insofar as they relate to mythology—have been selected as the illustrations for this book.

If the pictures are few, it is because the visualization of Indian myth is intended to be kept primarily in the minds of the listeners, who take their cues from the storyteller. Deadpan narration, typical of the modern non-Indian performance, is rare. Shouts, whispers, sound effects, and hand motions provide the usual signals, as narrator and audience inspire one another. Together they bring the story alive.

Part One↴

NORTHWEST COAST

One ↘

The Hungry Heroes

"Still it's the same"

In Tlingit country it was once claimed that only the rich told Raven stories, because only they had the time to learn them. On the other hand, modern Tlingit, who still tell the stories, have said that Raven thinks of the poor, just as Jesus did. Different as they are, the statements both ring true if it is remembered that the Tlingit today, like other Northwest Coast tribes, struggle to preserve remnants of their cultural heritage, while a single Tlingit mask of the classical period can bring tens of thousands of dollars at auction in New York.

Like the mask, the fully developed Raven myths belong to the second half of the nineteenth century. This was the time when rich chiefs, made richer by trade goods, built two-, three-, and four-street towns studded with totem poles—putting the crowning touch on what has been called the world's most elaborate nonagricultural society. Chiefs, nobles, and commoners all knew their places in a web of life that included full-dress warfare and professionalism in the arts. People of means counted their wealth in blankets, canoes, bracelets, and feasting dishes, as well as myths.

Though shorter and less frequently told than they once were, myths are still treasured. In publishing a new version of the Tsimshian Raven cycle in 1977, the native editors characteristically referred to the stories as "wealth." Raven myths may no longer give proof of personal status, but they do form a valuable link with the past. Comparing the modern Tlingit cycle with the classical version collected by John Swanton at the turn of the century, one storyteller commented with satisfaction that it was "a bit different—still it's the same."

Food and property

Raven stories are a characteristic feature of Northwest Coast culture, and even though everyone knows that Raven is a trickster, he is also the principal hero, at least for the northern group, which means the Tlingit, the Haida, and the Tsimshian. A second hero, called the Transformer, counts for little in the northern area but becomes increasingly important southward, until with the Kwakiutl he replaces Raven as the key figure.

Except in rare, atypical episodes, neither Raven nor the Transformer seems interested in the quest for wealth that colors so much of Northwest Coast lore. Rags-to-riches themes are plentiful throughout the region, and in the three northern tribes we meet the spirit called Property Woman, known by her curly gray hair. Whoever was lucky enough to catch sight of her or hear her child cry became rich. The Haida, in addition, had a spirit bird

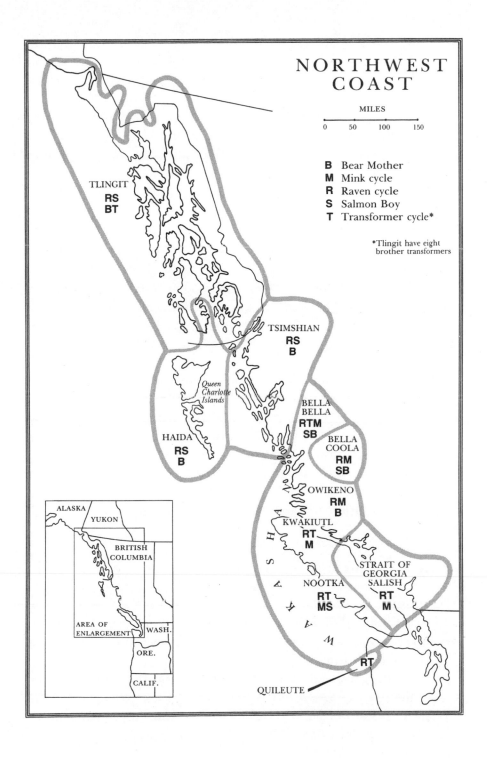

NORTHWEST COAST

MILES

0   50   100   150

B Bear Mother
M Mink cycle
R Raven cycle
S Salmon Boy
T Transformer cycle*

*Tlingit have eight
brother transformers

TLINGIT
RS
BT

TSIMSHIAN
RS
B

*Queen
Charlotte
Islands*

BELLA
BELLA
RTM
SB

BELLA
COOLA
RM
SB

HAIDA
RS
B

OWIKENO
RM
B

KWAKIUTL
RT
M

STRAIT OF
GEORGIA
SALISH
RT
M

NOOTKA
RT
MS

RT

QUILEUTE

ALASKA
YUKON

BRITISH
COLUMBIA

AREA OF
ENLARGEMENT   WASH.

ORE.

CALIF.

called Property, whose voice rang like a bell. Again, whoever heard it became rich. But the culture heroes, apparently, breathe a different air.

Raven's preoccupation is hunger. While it is true that tricksters everywhere tend to overeat, Raven outdoes them all. As for the Kwakiutl Transformer, his cycle typically begins with a story about eating.

Since food was the ultimate source of wealth and therefore the means, if indirectly, of acquiring property, it would be easy to conclude that the heroes' adventures have this as a hidden meaning. But if Franz Boas was correct in supposing that Northwest Coast tribes were sometimes brought to the brink of starvation, the mythical food quest could simply be taken at face value. Boas' conjecture, however, derived from no other source than folktales, and these contrast sharply with eye-witness accounts of a superabundant economy, based on the best natural fisheries in North America.

Indeed, the expert on Tlingit culture, Frederica de Laguna, links Raven's proverbial appetite with harsh food taboos in the midst of plenty. It is well known that fishermen did not take food while out on the water and that hunters fasted for days before an important expedition. Perhaps for reasons like these, inherited from the past, modern Tlingit continue to find Raven's gluttony significant and amusing. Interestingly, the quest for food is ridiculed throughout this lore; the quest for property, never.

The Raven cycle

Among the outstanding series of Raven tales is the one compiled by the bilingual Tsimshian Henry W. Tate, shortly before his death in 1914. Typically, Tate's cycle begins with the story of how Raven became hungry.

The world was still dark at that time, and the animal people were living in a town at the southern tip of the Queen Charlotte Islands. These people had a chief, whose son—an overprotected boy—fell sick and died. The boy's parents wailed day after day, insisting that everyone else join in their grief. One morning, however, the mother went to the loft bed where her son's body had been lying and saw a young man bright as fire. "Heaven was annoyed by your constant wailing," he said, "so He sent me down to comfort your minds."

The parents were overjoyed, believing their son had returned to them. But after a while they began to worry, because the shining youth refused to eat. The mother was afraid that without food he would die again.

Although it seemed that no one could awaken his appetite, the young man had noticed two slaves in his father's house who ate great quantities of food, and it made him curious. These slaves, male and female, were named Mouth At Each End.

"Don't desire to be as we are," warned the female. But the male, when it had been explained that the slaves whetted their appetites by tasting scabs, scraped a scab from his own leg and served it to the young prince in a dish of whale meat.

After that, the boy did nothing but eat until the town's store of provisions was nearly used up. Ashamed, the chief called his son to him, gave him a raven skin to wear, and named him *Wigyét* (giant). Then he handed him a bladder filled with seeds and told him to fly to the mainland and sow berries on the hillsides and fish eggs in the streams, so that he would always have plenty to eat.

He also gave him a round stone to use as a resting place in case he should be tired. On the way over, Giant dropped the stone on the water and it became a large rock, where he rested before continuing his flight.

The cycle continues with the well-known Theft of Daylight. According to this story, Giant, after scattering the fish eggs and the berries, decided it would be easier to get food if the world were not so dark. Knowing that light was kept in heaven, he flew up through the clouds as a raven and found the daughter of the chief of heaven about to drink from a bucket. He changed himself into a cedar leaf, floating in the bucket, and as the girl drank, she swallowed him and became pregnant.

In this way Giant was born into the house of the sky chief and was able to steal daylight, which hung from the ceiling in a box. Upon returning to earth, he found frog people at their night fishing and demanded that they throw him a candlefish. When they refused, he broke open the box, to spite them, and the world was filled with light. Thereafter, people called him *Chémsem.*

The third story in Tate's cycle concerns the origin of human mortality. As *Chémsem* wandered on, he met Stone and Elderberry, arguing over who would give birth first. To settle the matter, *Chémsem* touched Elderberry and she delivered. For this reason people die soon, and elderberries grow on their graves. If Stone had been the first mother, we would have been imperishable.

Tate's fourth story is a variant of The Theft of Fire, in which *Chémsem* disguises himself in a deerskin and returns to his father's village as the fire thief. After this, there is a euphemistic little tale in which the animals compete to see which of them can pull the sinews from his own belly and make them into a rope long enough to haul in sea eggs for *Chémsem* to eat. Tomtit wins and is rewarded by being made chief of the animals. Presumably this story has to do with the origin of sexual relations. (More explicit tales, in which Wren is the long-distance lover, have been recorded farther south.)

The sixth story accounts for the origin of low tide, so that shellfish can be gathered; and in the seventh through tenth, *Chémsem* obtains candlefish and learns how to cook it.

Stories eleven through thirty-six are trickster tales with seemingly less elevated consequences. Violence and ribaldry set the tone, along with the indispensable gluttony. In the final story, *Chémsem* invites all the monsters to a feast on a distant island, where he changes them into stones. He himself becomes a raven-shaped stone. In an epilogue, however, it is suggested that *Chém-*

A perch, or "sleeping pole," of Raven, formerly the property of the Tsimshian chief Quawm, mid-Skeena River, British Columbia. The human figures, called "people around" or "children," are a common feature of Tsimshian totem poles.

sem still lives somewhere beyond the mountains to the east and will give food to the wanderer who stumbles on his lair.

So brief a summary can do no more than suggest the main themes in Henry Tate's epic, which runs to 25,000 words in the English translation. The newer, 1977 version, called We-gyet Wanders On, is less than half as long but covers some of the same ground, including the origin of the hero's hunger and The Theft of Fire.

Tate's characterization of the hero's father and his mention of Heaven, or the chief of heaven, barely hint at a power higher than Raven. It will also be noticed that there is no creation of earth, unless the curious incident of the stone dropped on the sea can be said to serve that purpose. In general, Northwest Coast mythology downplays the cosmic and the mystical. These aspects are developed, however, in the old Haida variants, which storytellers called *Hoyá Káganas* (raven traveling).

One version begins: "From where we are now there were five villages [underworlds] below us. From where we are now there were five villages above us. [Pause. The narrator repeats the two statements.] Listen to what I am about to say.

"There was no land. There was only one chief who had a house. This was under water. He would always lie down with his back to the fire, which burned crystals. He was all alone. His name was Wonderful Doer."

The story continues with the entrance of the chief's assistant, Loon, crying because the supernatural beings had no place to settle. In answer, the chief removed a speckled rock and a white rock from the innermost of five nested boxes and handed them to Loon, who put them into the water. Bubbles came pouring from the two rocks, which formed the Queen Charlotte Islands and the mainland.

Then the chief lay on his back with his hands on his face and made the motions of catching something in them. "He blew on

---

The human face of Raven on a house post in the Raven House, Kluckwan, Alaska. Tlingit.

them, and a small object like a human being appeared in them. He stood it up and drew it upward until it became of full size. 'Now go and travel on the islands,' he said." And with this, Raven began his adventures. In another, similar version, the chief says to Raven, "I am you."

Few would doubt that this turn-of-the-century myth is of Indian invention. Whether it was current before the Haida received their first Christian mission in 1876 is a different matter. The myth's details are not Christian at all. But if its purpose is to rival the dogma of God the father and God the son, it succeeds admirably. Failure to consider such a possibility would be to underestimate the subtlety of native intellectuals and the rapidity with which new ideas are absorbed. Yet the question can only be raised, not answered.

We do know that Northwest Coast peoples today have accepted the doctrine of God in Christ and that those who attempt to bridge the gap between the new and the old use Raven as the medium. In contrast to the Transformer, who has faded with the passing years, Raven continues to spark interest, not only because tricksters are universally appealing, but because Raven is believed to be Godlike, the servant of God, or the equivalent of Jesus.

The Transformer cycle

Although Raven is often called a "transformer," especially in older writings, the term applies more comfortably to a different kind of hero, known also as the Reformer or the Changer. This figure is less of a creator than Raven, seldom a trickster, typically a deliverer, and at least sometimes fully human.

The highly variable Transformer cycle is popular in all areas bordering the Northwest Coast, but within the region it commands attention only in the south. Among the Quileute the Transformer was *Kweheti,* and it was said that he traveled all over, setting things right. The Salish tribes along the Strait of Georgia called him *Hals,* whereas the Wakashan, including the Kwakiutl, knew him as *Kánekelak*. A clue to his high standing among the Kwakiutl is that he often had encounters with clan ancestors, who thereby won prestige for their lineages.

As children, *Kánekelak* and his little brother were said to have been made hungry by their father, Heron, and their cruel, red-headed stepmother. One morning, after the parents had gone to the river and pulled a salmon out of the trap, the father said to his wife, "How can we keep the children from seeing this salmon and asking for food?" "Scare them," said the woman. So the father cried, "Children, run! Ghosts are coming!" and the little boys ran into the woods. Then the parents roasted the salmon as fast as possible and ate it before the children returned.

The next day there were two salmon in the trap, and again the boys were frightened away. The third day there were three salmon, and the fourth day there were four. But this time *Kánekelak*, peeping through a crack in the side of the house, saw his parents eating the roasted fish, two apiece, and heard his father say, "Finish it quickly, then we'll hide the bones." Rushing in, he seized the father and threw him into the air, saying, "You will be the heron of later generations." Then he threw the stepmother, and she became the redheaded woodpecker.

Now that they were alone, *Kánekelak* renamed his brother, calling him Only One, and built him an enormous new house to live in. Wearing a double-headed serpent as his belt and with the serpent's eyeballs as slingstones, he killed four whales and left them for Only One to eat. Then he started on his adventures.

As he went along, he saw the man called Deer sharpening a mussel shell, and he asked him what he was doing. "Don't you know?" said the man. "*Kánekelak* is coming to set things right. This will be my weapon in case he hurts me."

"Very well," said *Kánekelak*, "but this will be better." Then he put a mussel shell on each of the man's ears, saying, "You will be the deer of later generations," and the deer, with its mussel-shaped ears, jumped and ran into the woods.

The cycle goes on indefinitely with episodes of this sort, in which the dangerous animal people of the myth age are transformed into the ordinary animals of today.

In another kind of adventure, *Kánekelak* obtains supernatural power from one of the familiar monsters of Northwest Coast lore. In addition to the double-headed serpent, who becomes his belt, there is the dangerous thunderbird, also the cannibal woman who carries off children in her pack basket (called Woman of the Woods by the Nootka, *Tsúnukwa* by the Kwakiutl).

In further episodes, *Kánekelak* meets the clan ancestors—or sometimes avoids them, fearing their power. He may unsuccessfully challenge their ability at magic, acknowledge talismans that they wear, or show his favor by changing them into monumental boulders or a river teeming with fish. Such incidents clearly establish the antiquity of the lineages. Naturally, each clan has its own version.

At last *Kánekelak* returns to the great house he had built, where he finds that Only One, long since out of food, has become dry bones. But the hero has his water of life (the magic wand of Wakashan lore), and with this he revives his dead brother. His adventures done, *Kánekelak* retires to the south, sending Only One to live in the far north.

Sometimes it is stated that Only One does "bad things," such as sending disease from his home in the north, and in one variant his original name is Foolish With Property. Old-time narrators agreed that *Kánekelak* loved his brother dearly. Nevertheless, he allowed him to die. In these sketchy details we have what appears to be a rare Northwest Coast example of the mysterious dying god theme, not nearly so well developed here as it is in the Midwest and Southwest.

Mink

The disreputable side of the hero, represented by *Kánekelak*'s little brother and by Raven at his worst, comes through undiluted in the trickster Mink, whose appetite is mainly sexual, though he has a great fondness for eating sea eggs (the soft flesh of sea urchins). Mink ignores warnings, is unable to concentrate for more than a few moments, and tells lies habitually. He even smells bad.

Once popular in the southern half of the Northwest Coast region, the Mink cycle tends to dwell on the trickster's failed marriages with spirit women of the myth age. His most noteworthy adventure, however, is his trip to the sky, where he temporarily plays the role of the sun in a tale reminiscent of the Greek myth of Phaeton.

Mink, according to the story, was the son of a virgin who had been impregnated by sunlight filtering through cracks in her house. Much later, when confronted with his child, the sun hesitated, then remembered: "Ah, ah, ah, indeed! I obtained him by shining through." At Mink's insistence, the sun loaned him his mask and his earrings and permitted him to walk across the sky in his place, but with the warning that he must not sweep too much. Mink swept continually. That is, he brushed the clouds away, and as a result the earth grew so hot that forests burned and the sea began to boil.

Thus Mink was responsible for the world fire, a mythic event of minor significance along the Northwest Coast and in other parts of the continent, figuring prominently in the mythology of only one region, California.

Two ↘

Clans, Crests, and Ceremonies

The potlatch style

Caught up in the pursuit of riches, Northwest Coast chiefs and their retainers developed a form of polite warfare in which symbols as well as goods were the weapons. Competing chiefs represented their clans, who were as eager to display their genealogies, emblems, and knowledge of ceremonies as to prove that they could outspend their rivals.

The normal arena for these displays was the potlatch, a kind of assembly for the purpose of distributing wealth. The name comes from the Nootka word *patshatl*, meaning "gift," or "giving," which continues to be appropriate for the potlatches held today in villages up and down the coast. Guests no longer sit on cedar bark mats, and traditional feast foods such as salmonberries and candlefish oil have given way to coleslaw and roast turkey. But gifts are still handed out, and at the close of the doings someone may stand up and read a list of donors' names, including the dollar amount of each contribution.

Ceremonial masks, songs, and dances are still displayed at potlatches, recalling the days when a Kwakiutl chief could step forth and utter the cry of the *Tsúnukwa,* "Ho, ho, ho, ho!," then continue: "You all know, Kwakiutl, who I am. My name is *Yékalenlis.* The name began at the time when our world was made." To appreciate such taunts, it was necessary to know the myths that were being invoked. These were the charter myths that established ceremonial privileges and told of the origins of clans.

In potlatch oratory, especially as practiced by the Wakashan and the Bella Coola, the giving of gifts made a man's name "bright." Gifts were said to have "flowed away" or to have "become nothing" for the sake of the name. A man became "heavy" by giving many gifts, which "flattened" the name of his rival. If a host was lavish with his property, it was said that he "built up the fire" in his house. But the guest who outdid him "put out the fire." Figurative expressions like these, along with lists of privileges and descriptions of ceremonies, found their way into the charter myths, giving them a somewhat different quality from the trickster and Transformer cycles.

The House of Myths

The Kwakiutl chief who boasted that his name began "when our world was made" referred to the myth in which his first ancestor came down from the sky, took off his bird mask, and became a man. This was one type of ancestor myth in use among the Kwakiutl. Among the Bella Coola it was the only type, and all such narratives were said to be stored in a house above the sky called *Nusmatta,* the House of Myths.

In the beginning there were no living creatures except *Alkun-tam,* the supreme deity, who lived in *Nusmatta.* Deciding that he would populate the world, he created four supernatural carpenters who in turn made workers, who chiseled the first ancestors out of wood. The workers also chiseled and painted all animals, birds, trees, flowers, mountains, rivers, stars, and, in short, every feature of the universe except the sun, which seems to have been identified with the preexisting *Alkuntam.*

Around the walls of *Nusmatta* hung bird and animal cloaks, which the Creator invited the ancestors to wear. As one selected the eagle, another the grizzly bear, and so on, each became the bird or animal he had chosen. Then *Alkuntam* gave them their personal names and sent them down to earth, where each one landed on the peak of a mountain. Shedding their disguises, they resumed human form, and the cloaks floated back up to *Nusmatta.*

With this as background, family groups elaborated their own legends. One story, from the village of Nuskelst, begins with the statement that the first member of the lineage descended from *Nusmatta* with a special gift from the Creator—a model of the House of Myths itself, which the ancestor set up on earth as his own residence. This wonderful house lengthened of its own accord whenever a potlatch was held there. In front of its door lay a man with a huge stomach, which had to be stepped on by anyone who entered. If a commoner came in, no sound was heard. But when a mighty chief stepped on the stomach, his weight drew forth a grunt.

For the most part the clan stories of the Bella Coola and their neighbors tell of male ancestors. But the more northerly tribes, whose kinship systems were exclusively matrilineal, took a different view. The Tsimshian and the Tlingit simply did without clan origin myths. They had clan histories, but they did not trace their lineages back to the myth age. The Haida, however, recognized two mythic mothers, one each for the halves, or moieties, into which Haida society was divided. On one side were the several Eagle clans, descended from the Weeping Woman; on the other were the Raven clans, whose lineages began with Foam Woman.

The Weeping Woman, also known as *Djilákons,* is the subject of conflicting legends, some of which tell how she took the form of a frog, whom a party of hunters offended. In retaliation she destroyed all the people with a shower of volcanic fire, protecting one girl, who became the ancestor of the Eagles. In other versions, the Eagle clans are said to have emerged one after another from the womb of *Djilákons* herself. Foam Woman, by contrast, appeared at the time of the world flood. She had twenty breasts, ten on each side, and at each breast she nursed the future grandmother of one of the Raven families.

These stories of *Djilákons* and Foam Woman date from the classic period. But in the 1970s, even Haida young people, who disregarded most native traditions, were conscious of being either Eagles or Ravens.

Crest stories

Like the Haida, the Tsimshian and the Tlingit pass the clan name from mother to child. In former times a man owning property, which might include lullabies, personal names, hunting grounds, and bathing places, bequeathed it to his sister's son, since he and his own son belonged to different clans. Among the most valued possessions were the decorative clan emblems, or crests, roughly equivalent to the heraldic crests of European families. The "totem" poles that stood in front of great houses were actually crest poles, depicting whatever emblems the family had a right to display. All Northwest Coast tribes had stories explaining how a particular clan acquired the beaver, the eagle, the raven, or the killer whale emblem, to name only a few, and these could be used to adorn anything from blankets to spoons, as well as crest poles.

Perhaps because they lacked clan origin myths, the Tsimshian and the Tlingit developed the region's most noteworthy crest myths, often reshaping a romantic folktale to suit the purpose. In keeping with their matrilineal kinship systems, they favored heroine tales.

In the Tlingit story of the woodworm crest, a chief's daughter is said to have secretly kept a pet woodworm, feeding it different oils until it was as long as a man's outstretched arms. She composed two lullabies for it:

It has a face already
Sit right here
Sit right here

It has a mouth already
Sit right here
Sit right here

People could hear her singing in her room. She came out only to eat, then went back immediately. No one knew she was raising a pet. One day her mother spied on her and saw something large between the storage boxes. It seemed horrible to her. But she knew her daughter was fond of it, so she left it alone.

Meanwhile the people of the town began missing oil, because the worm was now stealing from them. The mother would say to her daughter, "Why don't you have something else for a pet?" But the daughter would only cry. She called the pet her son.

At last the people decided to kill the worm and begged the girl to come out of her room. For a while she refused, then finally gave in, singing a song that included the words, "I have come out at last, you have begged me to come out."

When told that her "son" was dead, she sang another song, ending with the words, "Although I am blamed for bringing you up, you will be claimed by a great clan and be looked up to as something great." From that time on, the four songs composed by the chief's daughter were sung by the *Ganatédi* clan whenever they were feasting, and the woodworm became one of their crests.

So strange a story will seem less strange, perhaps, if it is placed in the wider context of Pacific Coast folklore. In a tale told by the Achomawi of northern California, for example, Woodworm is a

Woodworm house post from the Whale House, Kluckwan, Alaska. Tlingit.

shy, inoffensive young man—and very handsome. The full story of the young woman who harbors a fingerling until it becomes a monstrous serpent recurs among the Coos Indians of Oregon, where the beloved pet is said to have brought home so much food that the girl's family became rich. Among the Tlingit themselves the story was well known, and at least one variant was collected as late as the mid-1950s.

Origin myths of the Winter Dance

Northwest Coast ceremonialism reached its highest development among the Wakashan tribes, who set aside the entire winter for the staging of dramatic rituals, or dances, known collectively as the Winter Dance. The theory behind many of these ceremonies was that a supernatural, such as the *Bukwus* (known in English as Wild Man of the Woods) or the Grizzly Bear spirit or the cannibal *Pápakalanósiwa,* had kidnapped a human being and had imbued him with its fierce, uncontrollable nature. The victim (actually an initiate into the mysteries of the Winter Dance) then had to be rescued and "tamed" before rejoining normal society.

Only the nobility could afford to be initiated with the pomp that such rites required. Ceremonial knowledge was therefore a mark of prestige. In effect, the Kwakiutl chief who introduced himself at a potlatch by sounding the cry of the cannibal *Tsúnukwa,* another of the Winter Dance spirits, was calling attention to his high rank.

Evidently the *Tsúnukwa*'s power to bring back the dead outweighed her proverbial dim-wittedness (hers was a slow, sleepy dance). In one of the Winter Dance origin stories, a fearless young hero, endowed with a sixth sense, helps a distressed *Tsúnukwa* recover the body of her dead son. After reviving the son with her water of life, the mother is so grateful to the hero that she gives him a supply of the water and a mask representing herself, which he later wears in performing the first *Tsúnukwa* dance.

Of higher rank were the *hamatsa* rites, said to have originated with the Owikeno tribe, where they were sanctioned by the tale of *Pápakalanósiwa*, a much fiercer cannibal than the *Tsúnukwa*. According to one of the older Owikeno versions, a young woman is kidnapped by this monster, becomes his wife, then helps her family establish the *hamatsa* dance following her rescue.

The woman is supposed to have been a chief's daughter, who disappeared while berry picking. In search of her, the chief's three sons traveled into the mountains, arriving easily at the house of *Pápakalanósiwa*, which they recognized by its rainbow-colored smoke. Inside they saw their sister rocking a little boy in a cradle.

As they entered, the child cried loudly, because the second brother had torn his leg on a thorn and the child wanted the dripping blood. "Scrape it off, please," said the sister. So he scraped it off on a stick and gave it to the child, who greedily licked it up.

Frightened, the brothers decided to leave, pretending they were only stepping outside for a moment. When they failed to reappear, the young woman rushed through the door, calling, "*Pápakalanósiwa*, there was flesh in the house and it went out!" Immediately the cannibal appeared and began pursuing the brothers, blowing his whistle and shouting *hap! hap! hap!* (the traditional cry of the *hamatsa* dancer). But the oldest brother threw down a stone, and it became a mountain that blocked the cannibal's path.

Before long, the cannibal was close behind them again. This time the brother threw a comb, which became a thicket, next a kelp bladder filled with oil, which became a lake, and finally a stick that changed into a huge cedar—giving them just enough time to get inside their father's house and bar the door.

Shouting through the door, the quick-witted chief promised he would kill his three sons and serve them as food if the cannibal would come back the next morning with his wife and child. This was agreeable. But when the cannibal returned, he and his child were seated next to a concealed fire pit, into which they tumbled.

When the bodies had burned, the chief's daughter, now returned to her senses, fanned the ashes, and as they flew upward, they turned into mosquitoes. "You shall be man-eaters forever," she said. "You will constantly be seeking man's blood." Then her mother found the cannibal's whistle, which had rolled to one side. "Oh," said the daughter, "I thought that had burned. Now we can have a winter dance."

Today the Winter Dance as an institution, with its sacred season and numerous ceremonies, has long since lapsed. As for the myth of *Pápakalanósiwa,* Chief Simon Walkus, who died in 1969, was perhaps the last Owikeno to recite it. But *hamatsa* dancers continue to perform at Kwakiutl, if not Owikeno, potlatches, and *hamatsa* whistles of modern manufacture have lately been available for purchase from craft dealers. Like the persistence of clans and the occasional raising of a new totem pole, the *hamatsa* reminds native people of their Indianness and puts non-Indians on notice that native America remains culturally and politically alive.

Three ⌇

Family Ties

Salmon Boy

The Biblical passage "and let them have dominion over the fish of the sea" has often been pointed to as the source of a dangerous flaw in Western thought, not shared by Indians. Claiming "dominion" over nature, modern civilization puts human needs first, whereas the mythology of the Indian imposes a more balanced view.

The Indian idea, developed in the myths of many different tribes, is that the products of nature are persons, which must be treated with respect. At the close of the myth age, these beings became the animals and plants of today. Yet, beyond the prying eyes of ordinary society, they still exist as persons, inhabiting a not too distant world that has its own rituals and daily routines. As we learn from the myths, human access to this world is achieved through imagined ties of kinship, by which the natural product becomes a wife, a husband, a mother, or a son: in other words, a loved one.

For the Northwest Coast region the most vital of these relationships was with the salmon, especially the spring salmon but also the sockeye, the coho, the dog, and the pink. Harvested in the warm season, dried for winter use, these indispensable animals were to Alaska and British Columbia what corn was to the Southwest.

In a favorite story of the Raven cycle, the hero in human form takes the salmon as his wife. She comes to him as a beautiful woman, and whenever she dips her fingers in water, salmon are produced. All goes well until Raven commits the ludicrous mistake of keeping a section of salmon backbone for use as a comb (salmon bones must always be returned to the water to ensure the immortality of the species). To make matters worse, he curses the "comb" when it becomes entangled in his hair. Offended, the salmon wife swims away.

A more serious myth, typical only of the northern half of the region, is the tale known as Salmon Boy, in which a young man who offends the salmon is taken away from his parents and brought to the town of the salmon people. There he learns to respect them, becomes a salmon himself, and returns briefly, as a human, to teach his people.

According to a Haida version, the boy was hungry but scorned the fish his mother gave him to eat, insisting it was moldy. Afterward, while swimming with the other children, he drifted into deep water and drowned, and the salmon people, catching hold of his soul, carried it with them as they traveled home to their village out in the ocean.

These were the worn-out salmon, who themselves had become souls. But in their village they assumed human form, and behind the houses the boy could hear the sound of children playing in a stream. When hungry, he was instructed to pull one of the "children" from the water and roast it, returning the bones after eating the flesh. At nightfall, as the children came in from their play, one of them was crying with a pain in the eye. The boy was told to make certain he had returned everything to the water, and sure enough, when he looked along the bank, he found an eye, which he threw into the stream. Immediately the child stopped crying.

In the spring, when the salmon people journeyed back to the mainland, the boy went with them and was caught by his own mother. Noticing the copper necklace around his throat, she realized that the salmon was her son. Within two days a human head emerged from inside the salmon skin. After six more days the boy came out entirely, leaving the skin behind.

The boy became a shaman and performed great feats of shamanistic art throughout the season. Finally, when the old salmon came drifting back to sea, he caught an unusual translucent specimen, which he recognized as his own soul. He killed it with a sharp stick, and he, too, fell dead. Beforehand, he had instructed the people to return his body to the water. They now did so, and it turned around four times and sank from sight.

Speaking of this myth, a modern Tlingit once remarked: "The Fish Commissioner thinks he knows a lot about fish, but we know more. In the old days we used to take care of fish. There is a wonderful story that explains how we know about fish." But the non-Indian wants to know: Does it help? The answer is that it almost certainly does. If you knew you had to return every bone and every eye, you would think twice before taking more than you really needed.

Bear Mother

Evidently salmon were a source not only of food but of shamanistic power, much as the woodworm monster and the cannibal spirit were sources of social and ceremonial power. In the various myths, all three were embraced either as sons or as spouses.

Comparable stories about bears, wolves, killer whales, and other species are told throughout the region. But of these the bear is the most important, or at least the most widespread, forming the subject of myths and rituals found in nearly all parts of the continent. Like the salmon, the bear represents power as well as food.

One of two major bear myths of the Northwest Coast is the story of *Kats,* told by the Tlingit, with Tsimshian and Haida variants. *Kats,* a member of the *Tékwedi* clan, married a grizzly bear woman and had children by her. Later, when he returned to his human wife, the bear wife warned him to bring food only to his bear children. Because he broke this rule, the bears killed him, and thereafter the *Tékwedi* claimed the grizzly as a crest.

A much greater favorite is the myth called Bear Mother, told by the same tribes but with considerable extension into the Wakashan and Plateau areas. The heroine, a haughty young woman, is abducted by a grizzly or a brown bear and becomes the mother of his children. With his knowledge, she betrays him, sending a signal to her brothers, who become his killers. This, too, is often told as a crest myth. Attempts to account for its appeal range from Catharine McClellan's observation that it forces "a dreadful choice of loyalties" to Marius Barbeau's suggestion that the bear is performing an act of self-sacrifice for the "salvation of mankind."

In a Tlingit version told in English in 1954, the young woman, when she stepped in bear dung on her way home from berry picking, cursed the bear, calling it Fat Foot. As she walked on, the strings of her basket broke and kept breaking, until the other women got tired of waiting and went home without her. Then a young man appeared and told her to follow him.

After a while he turned around and said, "Look at my feet that you called so wide." She started tying tails from her gopher robe

---

Four scenes from the Bear Mother myth (front and rear views of an argillite carving attributed to Charles Edenshaw, Haida): (1) embrace of the woman and the bear, (2) mother in bear form with cub on her lap, (3) mother with cub at her breast, and (4) the bear carrying the woman to his den.

at intervals along the path. When they reached his den, she married him and had two cubs.

Her three brothers now followed her trail, throwing their thoughts ahead of them like arrows, which landed in the den of the bear. The bear picked them up and threw them back, and in this way he knew he was going to be killed.

Before the brothers arrived, the bear told his wife they should cut off his head and put it under a waterfall, so no birds could get it. Then he pointed and said, "Do you see that smoke in the distance?" She could not. So he passed his paw over her eyes and asked, "Can you see it now?" "Yes, I can see it." "That's where the children's grandparents are living. When I die, you are to take them there."

In other versions, after the father has been killed, the two children, instead of being taken to their father's parents, come home with their mother, where all three revert to the form of bears and kill the mother's brothers. Of importance to hunters are such instructions as what to do with the bear's heart, what prayers are to be offered, and what mourning songs are to be sung over its body—details that were often given in the older variants of this myth.

Contradictions

Within a single tribe, versions of Salmon Boy and Bear Mother can be not only different but conflicting. Ranging more widely through the region's mythology, we find that the various tales and cycles do not fit neatly together, even if plot differences are overlooked. Changes of focus are required as we move from creation by fiat, as in the Bella Coola myth of *Alkuntam*'s carpenters, to myths of the Transformer and to tales of spontaneous shape-shifting, such as Bear Mother.

One reason for the variety is that the clans develop their own mythologies as a mark of prestige. Another is that Northwest Coast storytellers tend to define myth very broadly. Among the Tlingit, for example, there are two kinds of stories, *tlagu* (of the long ago) and *ch'kalnik* (it really happened). If we were to consider every story that might be called *tlagu,* or myth, we would have to include what pass in other cultures for short stories, folktales, and epics, with all the opportunities for creative expression these labels imply.

The same situation exists outside the Northwest Coast but is no doubt intensified by the competition between clans that characterizes this region. Contemplating the "exuberant" diversity, Franz Boas, in a series of essays written between 1898 and 1933, conceded the possibility of a unifying principle, then grew skeptical, and finally rejected it. "It would seem," he wrote, "that mythological worlds have been built up, only to be shattered again, and that new worlds were built from the fragments."

Part Two

FAR NORTH

Four ⤸

Storytelling in the Arctic

Shortening the night

If myths offered the Northwest Coast a means of advancing one's social position, among Eskimos they served the purpose of killing time. Before the days of satellite TV, stories were needed, if for no other reason than to help fill the endless winter night.

At its best, this eminently practical approach to storytelling gave rise to a secular entertainment industry unexcelled by any other native American culture. Only among the Pueblos and perhaps the Iroquois was the art of fiction so highly developed, and only in the Southwest did music play so great a role.

The other side of the coin is that storytelling was widely used as a soporific. During the long night, while telling stories, Netsilik grandmothers cultivated a monotonous voice so that children would fall asleep more quickly. In Greenland, where professional storytellers lived through the winter by their art, the narrator's greatest triumph was to get his listeners to drowse. Before beginning his masterpiece, he would proudly announce, "No one has ever heard this story to the end."

The custom of getting through the winter with the help of stories was no doubt widespread in the far north, extending to the subarctic Athapascan tribes. In Koyukon households people used to get into their beds and pull up the covers before the narrator started. In total darkness (the lamp had been put out) the storyteller would recite tale after tale, ending each one with the formulaic expression "I have chewed off a good bit of the winter." During the telling, there would be a running commentary of exclamations, groans, and laughter, comparable to the response of an audience in a darkened theater.

Creation tales

Eskimo listeners will tolerate folktales and an occasional myth, but in general they expect to hear stories of realistic human situations. Outside of Alaska the widespread Indian concept of a myth age, when animals were people, is little developed. There are only the slightest hints of a transformer, and except in Alaskan Raven stories, evidently borrowed from the Northwest Coast, there is no full-fledged trickster or culture hero.

All but lost in a rich tradition of oral fiction and song, mythology as such reaches its lowest ebb along the arctic coasts of western Canada. Farther east, among the Iglulik and the Netsilik, myths fare only a little better. With characteristic sophistication, a Netsilik woman once explained to the Danish explorer Knud Rasmussen, "The earth was as it is at the time when our people began to remember."

Nevertheless, a choice, if small, mythology does flourish along

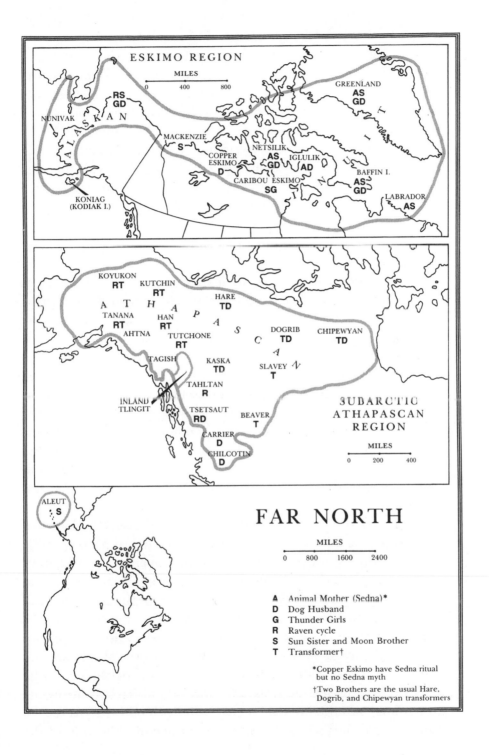

ESKIMO REGION

MILES
0   400   800

GREENLAND
AS
GD

NUNIVAK

A L A S K A N

RS
GD

MACKENZIE

S

COPPER
ESKIMO
GD
D

NETSILIK
AS
GD

IGLULIK
AD

I N U I T

BAFFIN I.
AS
GD

CARIBOU ESKIMO
SG

KONIAG
(KODIAK I.)

LABRADOR
AS

SUBARCTIC
ATHAPASCAN
REGION

MILES
0   200   400

KOYUKON
RT

KUTCHIN
RT

A   T   H   A   P   A   S   C   A   N

TANANA
RT

HAN
RT

HARE
TD

AHTNA

TUTCHONE
RT

DOGRIB
TD

CHIPEWYAN
TD

TAGISH

KASKA
TD

SLAVEY
T

TAHLTAN
R

INLAND
TLINGIT

TSETSAUT
RD

BEAVER
T

CARRIER
D

CHILCOTIN
D

ALEUT
S

FAR NORTH

MILES
0   800   1600   2400

A   Animal Mother (Sedna)*
D   Dog Husband
G   Thunder Girls
R   Raven cycle
S   Sun Sister and Moon Brother
T   Transformer†

*Copper Eskimo have Sedna ritual
but no Sedna myth

†Two Brothers are the usual Hare,
Dogrib, and Chipewyan transformers

these coasts, often in the form of miniature creation tales:

The Origin of Daylight. In the first times, when the land was still dark, Hare argued for light so he could find a place to feed, and Fox argued for dark so he could steal from people's food caches. Since Hare's words were more powerful, light came.

Male progenitors. After the world flood, two men emerged from the earth and lived as husband and wife. When the "wife" became pregnant, he sang, "A human being here, / A penis here. / May its opening be wide / And roomy. / Opening, opening, opening!" At this, the man's penis split with a loud noise, and he became a woman, giving birth to a child. From these three, mankind grew to many.

Thunder Girls. Offended by their irritable father, two girls ran away from home and entered the sky, taking with them a dried skin and a firestone. Whenever they shake the skin and strike the stone, it thunders and the sky glows.

Sun Sister and Moon Brother. A young woman had a lover who came to her bed after the lamps were out. One time she blackened her hands, and when the lamps were relit she saw that it was her own brother who had soot on his back. She accused him, picked up a torch, and ran outside. He pursued her with a dimmer torch, and the two rose into the sky, becoming the sun and the moon. (In an Aleut version they become hair seals. Although few Aleut stories have been recorded, an overall Eskimo quality seems unmistakable.)

The first of the four stories outlined above is a strictly Canadian myth, replaced by The Theft of Daylight in parts of Alaska, where it is one of the most popular tales of the Raven cycle. The story of the birth of people from two men, also Canadian, has an Alaskan counterpart in the local origin myth of the Nunivak, who tell of two brothers lost at sea. Frightened, the younger and weaker of the pair began to whine. *Sklúmyoa* (spirit of the universe) took pity on him and came down out of the sky, scattering something from inside her fishskin parka. This became Nunivak Island. Then she scattered something more, which became plants and animals. Suddenly the one who had whined discovered he had changed into a woman, who was to become the wife of the elder brother. From this pair were born the ancestors of the present Nunivak.

Sklúmyoa, the female Creator, is the supreme deity of the Nunivak, and prayers are usually addresssed to her. In Canada she reappears as *Sila,* also regarded as the spirit of the universe, though not as the supreme deity. *Sila* merely controls the weather.

The Alaskan Creator, however, is usually Raven. In the northern area, he establishes land by spearing a clod of earth and raising it to the surface of the primeval waters in a kind of simplified Earth Diver myth. Or, in a variant, he spears a piece of floating sod, "killing" it as though it were a hunted animal, whereupon it expands, forming land. In western Alaska, Raven creates the beach pea, from one of whose pods the first man emerges.

The same ideas are echoed in what is perhaps the most complex of all Eskimo creation tales, recorded on Kodiak Island in 1805 by the explorer Urey Lisiansky. Yet here Raven's role is greatly reduced.

As Raven secured light from the sky (method not given), a bladder descended, containing a man and a woman. These two stretched the bladder by blowing and pushing until it became the world. As they pushed with their hands and feet, mountains were formed. The man created trees by scattering his hair, and animals sprang up spontaneously in the forests. The woman made seas by urinating and produced rivers and lakes by spitting into ditches and holes; then she pulled out one of her teeth, the man turned it into a knife, and as he cut wood he threw the chips into the river to make fish. The couple's firstborn son played with a stone, which became an island. Another of their sons and a female dog were placed on the island and set afloat. This was Kodiak Island, and the present Kodiak people are said to have descended from this abandoned son and his dog wife.

The Kodiak story introduces several motifs found across the arctic to Greenland, including the creation of fish from wood chips and of bodies of water by urinating. The idea of tribal origin from the dog (one's constant companion in the arctic) is equally widespread, but the deed is usually blamed on a woman. The standard tale is the so-called Dog Husband, in which the woman is visited at night by a dog lover in human form, who becomes the father of her children. Alaskan groups allow the dog children to be their own ancestors, yet the proud Canadians have it that this was the origin of the Whites and the Indians—not the Inuit.

In the dialects of Eastern Canada and Greenland the word *inuit* (people) has always been used by Eskimos when speaking of themselves, and many prefer that non-Eskimos use it also. (Whether or not the term will be adopted in western Canada and Alaska, a political organization calling itself the Inuit Circumpolar Conference, representing all Eskimo groups, was applying in 1983 for nonvoting membership in the United Nations.)

The unity of Eskimo culture over an area extending nearly half the length of the Arctic Circle is one of the remarkable facts of native American life. The people speak a common language, exploit the same food resources, and share basic religious beliefs. In the realm of myth, though there are many local differences, this unity is preserved in tales like The Dog Husband, also Thunder Girls and Sun Sister and Moon Brother, which occur not only in Canada, as indicated above, but in Greenland and in Alaska.

The mother of animals

All regions except the Arctic have myths about game animals that suddenly disappear. A malicious spirit, or master of animals, has herded them into a cave, and it is up to the culture hero to find them and set them free. Among Eskimos this extremely important concept takes a different form, divided equally between myth and ritual.

The mythic part concerns a mistress of animals, who gives birth to game or in some way produces it from her body. Often portrayed in the myths as a rejected woman, she is vengeful and must be ritually placated. The release of the animals, never mentioned in myth, is—or was—accomplished through ritual. In Alaska, the bladders of game animals, saved up through the year, were inflated and set free in the ocean as the final act of the annual

Bladder Feast. The air-filled bladders represented the souls of the animals, which would return to be killed again. In the eastern arctic, where the Bladder Feast was unknown, the shaman made a trance journey to the undersea home of the animal mother, releasing the game that she jealously hoarded.

Animal mothers occur sporadically in the mythologies of both the Alaskan coasts and the subarctic Athapascan area. For example, on Kodiak Island there used to be a story about a young woman who gave birth to all the marine and land animals, one after another. Among the Hare Indians there was a mythical Egg Woman, who, after being abused and abandoned by human males, became the mother of the hares. In a myth of the Tahltan Indians, a pregnant woman, left behind by her migrating tribe, gave birth to moose, caribou, and all other animals, thus becoming *Atsentmá* (meat mother). People were careful not to offend her by breaking taboos, otherwise she would hoard the game.

The most celebrated of these myths is the story of the mistress of sea animals, found among the Iglulik and the Netsilik and eastward into Greenland. It is therefore an Inuit myth in the strict sense of the word. At its simplest, it tells of an unwanted woman thrown overboard, who clutches desperately to the gunwale as the man inside the boat chops off her fingers. These bob in the water and change into seals and walruses. Meanwhile the woman herself sinks to the bottom of the sea, where she becomes the ruler of the seals and the walruses and, according to some versions, of all other game as well.

Inuit storytellers occasionally explained that the woman was an orphan or a widow, whom no one would support. More often, however, they prefaced the basic myth with a folktale, using either The Dog Husband (in which the woman was the disgraced mother of the dog children) or a version of a common American tale that will here be called The Disappointed Bride. More a standard situation than a tale type, it concerns a young woman seduced by an animal lover in the form of an exceptionally handsome man. He takes her to his nest or den, where she discovers his true nature and strange way of life. Disgusted, she is eventually rescued by men of her tribe.

In the Inuit versions, the lover is a fulmar or a stormy petrel, who feeds his bride raw fish. When the disappointed girl's father comes to fetch her home in his boat, the bird raises such a storm by beating its wings that the father, to save himself, throws his daughter overboard. She then clutches at the gunwale, and so forth, becoming the mistress of animals.

In the best-known version, recorded on Baffin Island in the early 1880s, the woman's name is given as *Sedna,* and the story itself, in all versions, has come to be called the *Sedna* myth. In an associated ritual, held whenever game grew scarce, the shaman would make his trance journey in order to comb *Sedna,* whose hair had become infested with the vermin of broken taboos. Having no hands, she could not use a comb herself. As soon as the shaman had relieved her (and the people in the audience had confessed their sins), she would set the game animals free again.

Even beyond such rituals, the Inuit treated the animal mother as their supreme deity, who ruled over both *Sila,* the weather spirit, and Moon, the watchman who enforced taboos. In contrast to the more disjointed lore of Alaska, Inuit myth, ritual, and theology all focused on this single figure. In few religions is a goddess so unmistakably powerful.

Nevertheless, after the establishment of Anglican missions at the close of the nineteenth century, Inuit women were the first to abandon the native religion. Their men followed more slowly. Today in the southeastern part of Baffin Island, where the *Sedna* myth in its full form was first communicated to the outside world, all Inuit have become Anglicans, and the old rituals have been replaced by church services and evening Bible study.

Five ⤲

Athapascan Variations

The repeopling of the earth

Athapascan territory stretches from the Alaskan interior to within striking distance of the Columbia Basin and the northern Plains. The crest displays, masked dances, and potlatches of the west, with distance, change to the Plains-style vision quests of the south and east. In mythology, too, there is a gradual shift from Eskimo and Northwest Coast influences, as Raven, the trickster-hero of the far west, becomes a villain, then virtually disappears east of the Rockies.

A more or less consistent body of stories centering around the manlike Transformer gives the region its continuity. But perhaps the most characteristic theme is the sequence of flood, earth diver, and repeopling that crops up in both the Transformer and Raven cycles and also occurs separately, often with a council-of-animals motif.

An Athapascan twist is the idea of a world snowfall, which precedes the flood. Sometimes this is worked together with another motif of the region, the weather bags guarded by a monster bear. A Chipewyan myth collected about 1870 by the French missionary Émile Petitot illustrates one of the many possible combinations. According to this version, it snowed so hard one winter that the earth was covered to the tips of the tallest spruces. Led by the squirrel, the animal people climbed into the sky in search of warmth, and there, hanging in leather bags from a tree, were all the elements—rain, snow, fair weather, storms, cold, and warmth.

Working together, the animals were able to steal the bag of warmth from the bear who guarded the tree. But then, because the journey home was a long one, they had to make many camps. At one of the stops, the squirrel cut a tiny piece from the bag to patch his moccasins, and all the warmth rushed out, melting the snow.

The world was now flooded, but Old Man with his raft saved the animals in pairs, and from the raft they took turns diving. Finally a duck succeeded in bringing up a piece of mud, from which the entire earth was built anew.

In a variant told by a Tagish woman in 1979, the squirrel is portrayed as a female, worried that her children will freeze. After the bag of warmth has been stolen, the narrator concludes: "They bust it, the summer bag. Pretty soon snow melt, everything melt. They got leaves. They had all the leaves tied up in a balloon. They bust the balloon. And all the summer things came out."

Such rough and ready English comes from a woman for whom it is definitely a second language. But like other Athapascan storytellers at present, she prefers to speak to young people without having her words filtered through an interpreter. Although several northern Athapascan languages are still very much alive, and a few are even gaining speakers, Tagish is not among them. Convinced that myth has value for the younger generation, experienced narrators resort to English to make sure they will be heard.

The Transformer

The Athapascan Transformer is normally a deliverer, concerned with ridding the ancient world of man-eating animals. Called Wise One by the Hare, Navigator by the Kutchin, and Old Man by the Han, the Dogrib, and the Chipewyan, he is also identified with the beaver and widely known as Beaver Man, especially among the Tanana, Tutchone, Kaska, and Slavey. His style is to travel from place to place, typically by canoe.

Bear, Wolverine, Sheep, Woodchuck, and various stupid giants try to trap him and eat him, unsuccessfully of course, and if this were the extent of his adventures, the Transformer would be quite easy to understand. However, the situation is complicated by the Transformer's relationship with Raven and by the introduction of sexual themes more noticeable here than in either the Northwest Coast or Eskimo regions.

Raven, the trickster-provider-creator, has his own cycle of myths in the western areas, much of it borrowed from the Northwest Coast. The Theft of Daylight seems to be the most popular of these stories, and Raven is also the overseer in The Earth Diver. Moving into the central part of the region, where the cycle rapidly loses ground, we find Raven reappearing as one of the Transformer's adversaries.

The two are housemates in a myth of the Kutchin and the Hare. But Raven is such a thief that the Transformer, tired of being victimized, throws him into the fire—this despite Raven's warning that his death will cause humans to disappear. When the prediction comes true, the Transformer gathers Raven's bones, covers them, and breaks wind, and Raven revives. (Imparting the breath of life in this undignified manner shows the Transformer's own trickster tendencies.) Then the two go down to the riverbank, where the Transformer punctures a pike, and men come out, while Raven punctures another fish—the loche, or burbot—and women are produced. Thus the world is repopulated. In another tale, Raven hoards game or drives it away, and the Transformer has to release it. In stories like these the Transformer becomes a provider-creator.

One of the tacit assumptions of Indian storytellers is that the provider or creator may have sex, whereas the deliverer remains chaste. Since culture heroes tend to be providers as well as deliverers, this rule constantly gets mixed up, and many storytellers fail to observe it altogether. Nevertheless, even within a single myth cycle it is often possible to see that sex is linked to provider episodes, and celibacy, or even a violent abhorrence of sex, combines with saviorlike adventures.

The point is illustrated in the Athapascan arrow cycle, where the Transformer, in his role as monster slayer, confronts a cannibal who has a daughter. To test the hero, the cannibal first sends him to a thunderbirds' nest to get feathers for making arrows. Next he must make an attack on a giant elk to get sinews for binding the feathers to the arrow shafts. (The Visit to the Thunderbird Nest and The Attack on the Giant Elk, incidentally, are two important tales that were carried south by the Athapascan Navajo.) In further episodes the hero overcomes dangers in order to get wood for the shafts and paint to decorate the finished arrows. At last, when he has passed these "son-in-law tests," to use the term applied by folklorists, he shoots and kills the prospective bride.

But in a Kaska version, the storyteller decides to append a provider episode and so brings the murdered bride back from the dead. The Transformer then has his scrape with Raven, the game hoarder, and takes caribou meat home to his new wife.

In a number of these myths, the mink, the weasel, or the mouse symbolizes dangerous sexuality. In one story a temptress has both a mink and a weasel hidden inside her body, ready to bite an unwary lover. Not tempted, the transformer-deliverer kills the woman with a heated stone, then kills the murderous bodyguards.

In the eastern part of the region, stories of this nature are assigned to the so-called Two Brothers, who are rarely deliverers, usually providers. In a Two Brothers tale of the Chipewyan, the younger of the pair breaks a prohibition and is lured into the sky. There he weds two huntresses called Bosom of Weasels and Bosom of Mice. The moment he lies with them, he is automatically buried alive, and one of the women gives birth to mice, rats, and other "evil creatures," which spread disease, hunger, death, and cold over the earth.

Symbolic myths of death, food, and sexual love, inviting psychological interpretations, are of particular interest to mythologists and literary critics, if not to ethnographers. It may be added that such myths are most luxuriantly developed in the simpler cultures, such as those of the Athapascan, Plateau, and Great Basin regions—precisely the regions that have always been slighted in descriptions of North American myth and folklore.

The vision quest

Individuals in Northwest Coast societies gained supernatural power by having it thrust upon them. But Athapascans, especially in the eastern areas, were not accustomed to the elaborate ritual of being "kidnapped" by a dangerous spirit. They had to go out into the wilderness of their own accord and seek a spirit helper through dreams or visions.

Ordinarily the seeker was a boy at puberty, who hoped that the soul of an animal would appear to him and grant him its power, making him a successful hunter. Once he had acquired his vision, it would guide him through life, and if he needed to recapture the initial sensation, he might do so by dreaming or singing.

Such beliefs do not often encroach upon myth. Or if they do, their influence is so subtle that it goes undetected unless storytellers are willing to explain what meanings the myths have for people who use them. In the 1970s it came to light that the Athapascan Transformer cycle, as understood by the Beaver Indians of Alberta and British Columbia, incorporated the vision quest as a central theme. This would not be obvious without inside information.

The cycle opens with a modified Bird Nester story (the jealous father maroons his son on an island instead of leaving him in a nest), followed by a murder scene in which the dangerous woman is dispensed with, then trails off in the usual series of adventures in which the hero overcomes monster animals of the myth age.

At first the hero's name is Swan. He is a boy who has just reached puberty, old enough to bring home rabbits. But his provocative stepmother insists on going hunting with him. When he shoots a rabbit, she quickly places it between her thighs, so that it scratches her with its final few kicks. Later she lies to her husband, saying that Swan has molested her.

Angry, the father takes Swan on a hunting trip to a distant island and leaves him there alone. After crying himself to sleep, the boy hears a voice telling him to spread pitch on the flat rocks nearby. He takes the advice and finds that when game birds land on the gluey rocks he catches them easily. In this way he lives through the winter.

In the spring, when the father comes to gather up his son's bones, Swan seizes the canoe and leaves the father stranded. Returning home, he shoots an arrow at the stepmother, who tries to escape by running into the water. The arrow is hot, so hot that it boils the water, causing the flesh to fall from the woman's bones. Now the hero takes the name *Saya* (sun or moon—the word is the same for either) and travels around the rim of the world, transforming the monsters into the animals of today. Finally he himself changes into a stone, though it is said he will return in order to set things right when the present world comes to an end.

According to the people who have preserved this story, the hero's sojourn on the island was a vision quest. Boys who sought power therefore identified with Swan, and as they went out into the woods on their quests, they believed they would meet one of the outsized animals that Swan had met during his adventures as *Saya.* In spite of discrepancies between myth and practice, the interpretation shows how a story put together out of the common store of Indian tradition can become a sacred text, with special meaning for a particular people.

Copper Woman

Athapascans had access to two principal sources of native copper, one on the Copper River in Ahtna territory and the other on the Coppermine River, shared by the Chipewyan and the Copper Eskimo. Capable of being pounded into knife blades and other items, the metal was highly valued.

According to an old Ahtna legend, an outcast woman and her young son discovered copper nuggets while living together in the mountains. In a dream the boy heard a voice say, "If you see four blue flames on the fire, that's me." Later he saw the flames and dug copper out of the fire pit when the ashes had cooled. Thereafter, people looked for copper every spring but found it only if the boy's mother led the way.

Better known is the Chipewyan myth of the Copper Woman abducted by an Eskimo, who made her pregnant. Finally escaping with her infant child, she fled homeward across the "great water," led by a wolf. With her sewing awl she killed a caribou. Then, seeing that her little boy had the appetite of a monster, she abandoned him, continuing alone. Along the way she discovered yellow nuggets glowing like fire, and when she reached home she agreed to show the men of her tribe where to find them if they promised not to molest her. She led them to the spot, but they broke their promise, and she sank into the ground above her waist. Following her instructions, the men came back another time with an offering of caribou meat, only to find that both the woman and the copper deposits had disappeared into the earth. They left the offering anyway, and when they returned again they saw that the meat had become copper—all of it usable except for the part that had been the liver, which was too hard, and the part that had been the lungs, which was too soft.

The Dog Husband

The Athapascan Dog Husband differs somewhat from the Eskimo form of the tale, which has the young woman and her pups banished to an island. In one version of the Athapascan story, the

woman's brothers, realizing their sister has taken a dog lover, kill
the dog and drive the sister into the woods, where she gives birth
to six pups. Whenever her back is turned, the children become
human, changing into dogs again as soon as they know their
mother is watching.

The mother eventually catches three of them in human form;
the other three she destroys. Of the ones she keeps, two are sons,
who marry the third, a daughter, who becomes the ancestral
mother of the Dogrib. The Hare and the Chipewyan also trace
their ancestry to the dog children, but for most other Athapascans who tell this story it is merely a folktale, without ancestral
associations.

For the Chilcotin, the southernmost of the northern Athapascans, The Dog Husband serves as an introduction to the Transformer cycle—as it does for the Tlingit. In the Chilcotin version
the three pups that become human are all boys, who promptly set
out on the usual adventures. South of the Chilcotin, The Dog
Husband continues on as a popular folktale, if not as a myth,
through at least the northern half of the Columbia Basin. To the
east it survives here and there on the northern Plains, finally
fading out with the Cheyenne and the Arapaho.

Part Three ↳

SOUTHWEST

Six

The Emergence

Aztec echoes

Southwest mythology has two great creation epics, The Dying God and The Emergence, to which may be added a deliverer cycle on the theme of the hero who returns to his mother or grandmother. Stories that do not fit into one of these three patterns tend to become secular literature, including trickster tales and stories for young children. Since all three of the principal epics have parallels in old Aztec and Maya myths, it has often been assumed that Southwest traditions derive from Mexican and Central American sources.

The influence seems strongest in the western part of the region, where several groups speak Takic and Piman languages, which are related to the language of the Aztecs. Two favorite incidents, the cremation of the dying god and the theft of his heart, recall the cremation of the Aztec god Quetzalcoatl, whose heart rose to the sky after his body had burned. In addition, the form of the deliverer cycle called Flute Lure bears a resemblance to the hero cycle in the *Popol Vuh,* the national epic of the Quiche Maya of Guatemala.

Unfortunately, Indian mythology in the north of Mexico did not survive long enough to be recorded, so that the historical connections between the myths of the United States and those of Guatemala and the Mexico City area, if connections did exist, would now be hard to trace.

The Emergence, which is characteristic of the eastern half of the Southwest, has a southern parallel in the story of Aztec ancestors who emerged from seven caves, then migrated southward to found the Mexican capital. But the Southwest treatments of this theme are so much more elaborate that a case could be made for the Aztecs having received it from the north.

For many Indians in the United States, even beyond Arizona and New Mexico, The Emergence is the premier myth. People know it and respect it, just as Euro-Americans respect the Book of Genesis. This feeling extends to lawyers, teachers, novelists, and other professionals who have entered the mainstream of modern American life. For them the sacred text embodies a concept of profound religious significance, and many still treat it as an article of faith. One cannot speak of The Emergence as a relic of the Indian past.

Contrasting views

Although the Emergence story belonged to the Pueblos before the Navajo and the Apache received it, the available Navajo variants are easily the fullest and the most numerous. These usually describe a series of three or four underworlds, one on top of the

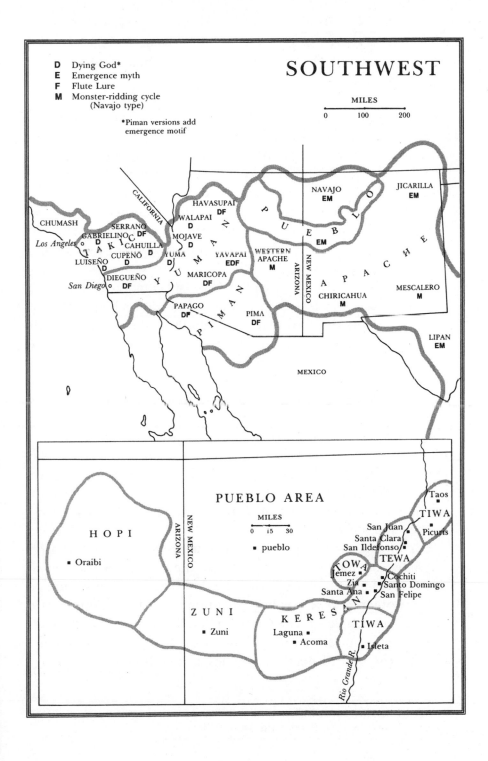

SOUTHWEST

D — Dying God*
E — Emergence myth
F — Flute Lure
M — Monster-ridding cycle
(Navajo type)

*Piman versions add
emergence motif

MILES
0   100   200

CHUMASH

Los Angeles

SERRANO
GABRIELINO
CAHUILLA
CUPEÑO
LUISEÑO
D
DIEGUEÑO
DF
San Diego

TAKIC

HAVASUPAI
DF
WALAPAI
D
MOJAVE
D
YUMA
D
MARICOPA
DF

YAVAPAI
EDF

WESTERN
APACHE
M

YUMAN

PIMAN

PAPAGO
DF
PIMA
DF

PUEBLO

NAVAJO
EM

EM

ARIZONA   NEW MEXICO

APACHE

CHIRICAHUA
M

JICARILLA
EM

MESCALERO
M

LIPAN
EM

MEXICO

PUEBLO AREA

MILES
0   15   30

■ pueblo

HOPI

■ Oraibi

ARIZONA   NEW MEXICO

Taos ■

TIWA

San Juan
Santa Clara
San Ildefonso
TEWA

Picuris ■

TOWA
Jemez ■
Zia ■
Santa Ana ■
Cochiti ■
Santo Domingo ■
San Felipe ■

ZUNI

■ Zuni

KERES

Laguna ■
Acoma ■

TIWA

Isleta ■

Rio Grande R.

other, through which the first beings passed before emerging at the earth's surface.

In the composite version agreed upon by a group of Navajo in the early 1970s, the first world is called Black World. Small in size, like an island floating in mist, this world was inhabited by ants and other insect people. Coyote was also there. Pairs of clouds touched each other, and First Man and First Woman came into existence. As yet, however, none of these people were fully human. Quarrelsome and dissatisfied, they emerged through an opening into the second world, where they found larger insects and dangerous mammals. The quarreling continued, and so they moved upward again.

In the third world, Coyote mischievously kidnapped the Water Monster's baby, with the result that flood waters began to rise. First Man planted a reed that grew rapidly to the sky; the people entered the reed, climbed upward, and emerged into the present, or fourth, world. The story then continues with a series of postemergence episodes, including the birth of the twin war gods, their campaign against monsters, and the establishment of the Navajo clans.

For the Navajo the journey upward was one of extraordinary difficulty. Two of the Navajo healing ceremonials, Red Antway and Upward-reachingway, refer extensively to The Emergence, with the idea of rescuing the patient from the contagious evils of the underworld. Significantly, Navajo versions of the myth stress danger and strife.

By contrast, the Hopi think of the Emergence myth as a charter for initiation into manhood. At first the beings in the lowest underworld live contentedly in a kind of paradise. Sex begins to cause problems. Wife-stealing is mentioned. Their simple world tainted, the people proceed upward, led by the twin war gods. As they emerge onto the surface of the earth, they are met by *Másawu* (ghost), the god of death, who shows them how to plant corn.

Emergence, acrylic, 1974, by Dawakema (Milland Lomakema, Sr.), Hopi. The painting hangs in the offices of the Hopi tribe.

Already familiar with simple versions of this story, boys learn the full form of the myth during the protracted puberty rites known as *wúwuchim*.

The Zuni also regard the telling of The Emergence as part of a young man's initiation. Once every four years, in April, the myth is supposedly brought up from the underworld by the messenger god *Kyáklo,* who chants a special, somewhat cryptic version. Carried by ten clowns, the *Kyáklo* impersonator must follow a fixed route into the village. (Since a subdivision now lies across the traditional path, the clowns have to go through people's yards and over the roof of one of the houses.) Initiates and others await his word in the ceremonial chambers called kivas. As in most of the Hopi variants, the Zuni story includes the twin war gods as leaders of the emergence.

East of Zuni, at Isleta and in the Keresan pueblos, Emergence stories emphasize the fertility of the underworld. Still farther east, among the Jicarilla Apache, the myth becomes an unmistakable allegory of gestation and birth, with underground swelling, and emergence through an opening at the top of a mountain. A Jicarilla narrator once commented, "When we came up on this earth, it was just like a child being born from its mother."

For the Isleta and the Keresan, however, the underworld is the home or the birthplace of two sister deities, one of whom is the Corn Mother. Usually these two are advised by a higher power, identified as either Thought Woman or Spider Woman. In one version Thought Woman, prior to the emergence, gives the two sisters baskets of seeds and images, representing all future beings. In another version the Corn Mother plants bits of her heart, from which corn is evolved; then she declares, "This corn is my heart and it shall be to my people as milk from my breasts."

In these eastern Pueblo variants there is only one underworld, rather than a series of three or four as in Zuni and Navajo lore, and the opening, or *sípapu,* is often believed to lie directly beneath a particular lake. Since most of the eastern Pueblos are secretive about their traditions, the published Emergence variants from this area are fragmentary and the locations of sacred lakes poorly charted.

The Taos, the most secretive and perhaps the most conservative of all Indian tribes, have divulged neither their Emergence myth nor details of the associated rituals. The emergence lake of the Taos, according to some reports, is the now dried "black spring" near Alamosa, Colorado; others mention Blue Lake, just ten miles northeast of Taos pueblo. As is well known, the sacred Blue Lake, to which young Taos men are taken as part of their initiation experience, was the subject of a historic piece of legislation approved by the United States Senate on December 2, 1970. On that date the Senate, with full awareness of the political if not the religious significance of this shrine, returned Blue Lake to the Taos along with 48,000 acres of surrounding forest lands.

Gods

The best-known gods of the Southwest are the kachinas, the masked gods of Pueblo ritual, who appear especially in dances of the winter season. These correspond to the western and southern Apache crown dancers, or *gáhe,* called *hastshín* by the Jicarilla and the Lipan. The masked *yéi,* featured in the Navajo Night Chant, are roughly comparable. Among the Zuni, kachinas and other spirits addressed in prayer are called *awonawillapona* (those who hold our roads). Such gods belong to ritual, not to mythology. Yet in many cases they encroach upon the Emergence myth, and a few have become firmly established as part of the story.

In an unusual but famous version of the Navajo Emergence, the *yéi* create First Man and First Woman by placing two ears of corn under a buckskin. Wind enters, and as Mirage People circle four times around, the corn becomes human.

The Hopi kachina *Másawu,* who greets the beings just arrived from the underworld, figures prominently in almost all versions of the Hopi Emergence. (In dances, the impersonator of *Másawu* wears a skeleton mask with enormous white eye sockets.) At Zuni and in the pueblos to the east, The Emergence frequently includes at least a brief episode that accounts for the origin of the kachinas as a group or establishes some aspect of their ritual.

In the beginning

Since it tells how humans, food, work, and nearly all customs
came into existence, The Emergence may be called a creation
myth, though it says nothing about the origin of the world itself.

As if to correct this omission, narrators sometimes introduce
the Emergence cycle with the description of a first cause. In the
Jicarilla version this is said to be the *hastshín,* who existed "in the
beginning" when there was nothing but Darkness, Water, and
Cyclone. In possession of the materials from which everything
would be created, the *hastshín* made the earth and the underworld
first, then the sky. In the underworld were all kinds of *hastshín,*
and from this place the emergence started.

As used here, the term *hastshín* does not refer to the masked
dancers but to the spirits, or personalities, that dwell in objects
and living things.

Similar myths once current at Zuni pueblo identified the first
cause with the *awonawillapona,* or gods addressed in prayer. In
one version it is recorded that *Awonawilona* (singular form of
awonawillapona) existed alone in the void. Out of his thoughts he
created mist, then made himself into the sun. Becoming thick, the
mist fell as rain, which formed the ocean.

Next, *Awonawilona* took some of his flesh and placed it on the
surface of the water, where it expanded into a scum that finally
assumed the shape of Mother Earth and Father Sky. Lying together, these two conceived all life in the four-chambered womb
of the earth, from which the emergence proceeded as in the usual
versions of the story.

Within the Pueblo sphere of influence, narratives of this type
were regularly produced only in Apache areas. In fact, among the
Chiricahua, the Mescalero, and the Western Apache, The Emergence itself drops out, and the narrative of the world's origin
leads right into the monster-ridding cycle.

Unlike the Pueblos, who use The Emergence in male initiation
ceremonies, the Apache relate their creation cycle to the girls'

puberty rite, an important tribal ceremony still held today. Among the Mescalero this annual rite, which prepares young women for motherhood, is believed to be responsible for the tribe's increase in population, from about five hundred at the turn of the century to more than two thousand in the 1970s.

A branching mythology

For the Navajo, The Emergence is a catchall that incorporates virtually all myths and folktales known in the Navajo language, except for comic tales of Coyote and stories about a character called Tooth-gum Woman. Myths are added either by fitting them into the main sequence of events or by branching off, typically at one of two points: just after the people have emerged from the lower world or just after the twin war gods have slain the monsters.

In theory, the origin myths of all the great Navajo ceremonials are contained in segments of these mythological branches. In order to account for any one of them in proper fashion, you must tell it up from the beginning, starting at the lowest underworld. The entire corpus amounts to one of the most impressive of all Indian mythologies, and certainly it is the most heavily documented, with many dozens of published volumes mapping out portions of the whole.

The ceremonials themselves are healing rites, each with its own procedures, songs, and curative sand paintings. Night Chant, Mountain Chant, Bead Chant, Shooting Chant, and Coyoteway are among the twenty-five or more that have been reported. For each there is an elaborate charter myth, usually about a hero who visits the distant home of supernaturals, learns the ceremonial, then brings it back to his tribe.

In practice, however, most ceremonial myths are not connected to The Emergence at all, or, if they are, the connection is suppressed. Sometimes a narrator will simply begin with "After the monsters had been killed . . ." or words to that effect. In the case of the Bead Chant story, one of the better known of the ceremonial tales, the connection is made by saying that the hero is "a boy of the first people created" or that he is the son of Bead Woman, who was born of Changing Woman (the mother of the twin war gods).

From a folkloristic point of view, the Bead Chant myth is a Bird Nester tale, incorporating another widespread story, The Visit to the Thunderbird Nest. Predictably, both the myth and its ceremonial recur among the Western Apache, whose rituals are more Navajo-like than those of any other Apache group.

The Bird Nester

The Western Apache do not speak of the "Bead Chant" but of the "ceremony to cure one who gets ill from eagle feathers when he uses them to put on his arrows." According to the origin myth of this ceremony, a man who had a wife and two young sons went off on a hunting trip with Coyote, and they camped the first night. In the morning, setting out by himself, Coyote noticed an eagle's nest halfway up a high cliff. There were young eagles in the nest.

Returning to camp, he told the man what he had seen and asked if he would help him reach the eaglets, saying he needed feathers for feathering arrows. The man agreed, and when they got to the cliff, Coyote began lowering him over the edge.

"Have you come to the eagles?"

"Not yet," he replied.

"Have you come to the eagles?"

"Yes."

Then Coyote let the rope fall on the man, saying, "Cousin, she who was your wife will be mine."

Opposite page and following two pages. Three scenes from the Bird Nester myth as shown in sand paintings of the Navajo Bead Chant: (1) the hero and two eaglets in the eagles' nest, surrounded by food animals, with parent eagles at extreme top; (2) the hero's ascent, with eagles; and (3) the eagles' home in the sky.

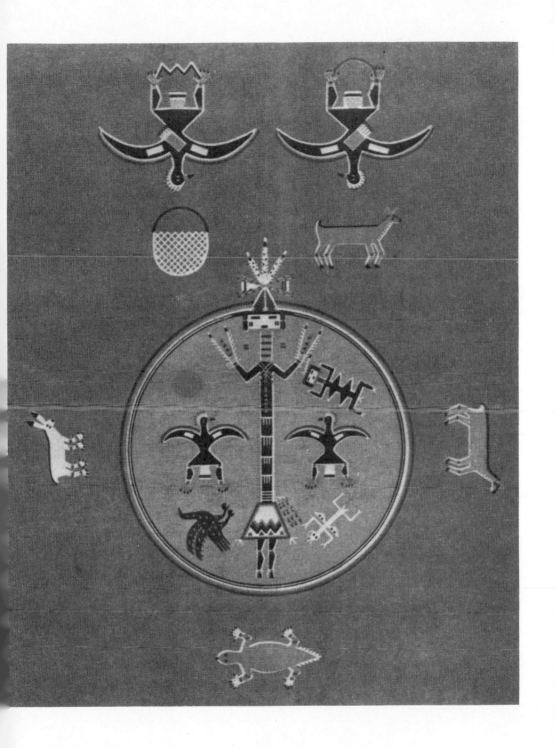

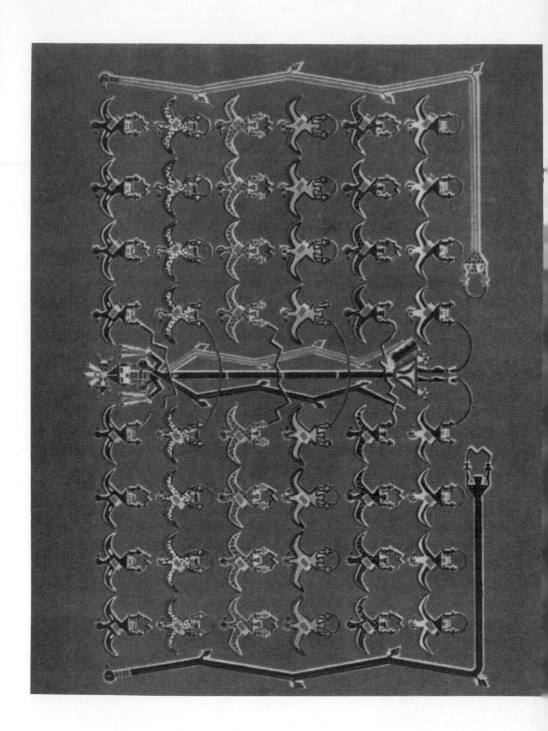

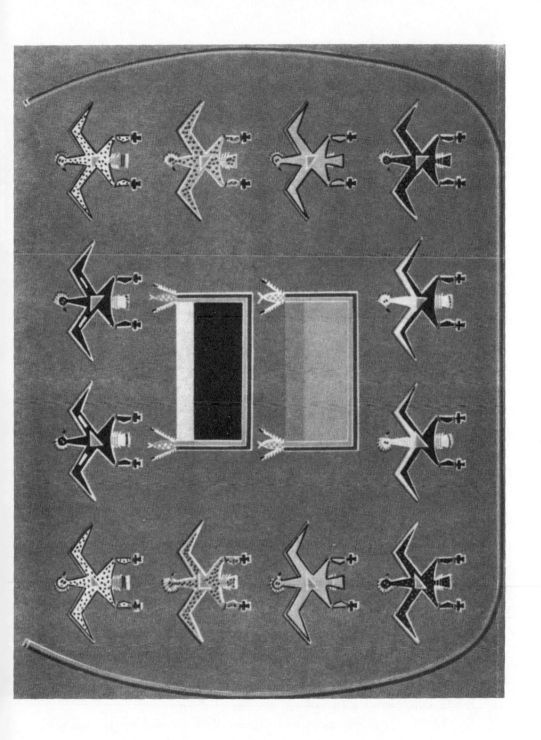

As the man sat in the nest with the eaglets, he asked them what kind of weather it would be when their father returned. They answered, male rain (rain with thunder), and soon the father appeared, accompanied by male rain.

When the man explained that Coyote had lowered him into the nest and that he would protect the eaglets from harm, the father told him he could stay, then flew off and came back with a turquoise drinking vessel, so that the man could have water. Later, the mother eagle arrived, accompanied by female rain (rain without thunder) and brought the man a dish of boiled corn that replenished itself automatically whenever he ate.

Four days later the eagle people all assembled. They gave the man an eagle shirt and told him to put it on. "Where am I going?" he asked. Then he sang:

> Where the black mirage is located at the center of the sky, I go up. In the
>   shadow of his dark wings I come.
> Where the blue mirage is located at the center of the sky, I go up. In the shadow
>   of his blue wings I come.
> At the center of the sky, I go up. In the shadow of the yellow wings I come.
> Where the white mirage is located at the center of the sky, I go up. In the
>   shadow of the white wings I come.
> Between the two who sit on the white sky, I go up. Where the white weeds tower
>   up, white on the sky at its center, I go up.
> Where the dark houses of the eagles project, I come.
> Where the blue houses of the eagles project, I go up.
> Where the red houses of the eagles project, I go up.
> Where the white houses of the eagles project, I go up.

When they had all reached the sky world, the eagles invited the man to come into one of their houses, but he refused. Instead, he went out into the night and killed "the one with a skull that kills coming." Then he killed bees that had stung eagles to death, then wasps and yellow jackets, and murderous tumbleweeds that had killed eagles by rolling on top of them.

When his adventures were done, the grateful eagles showed him how to fly back down to earth, where he found Coyote living with his wife and mistreating his two little boys. The wife had a bad odor from being with Coyote.

Taking revenge, he made Coyote swallow two hot stones that his wife had baked in the fire. But the man was no longer content to live on earth. Becoming an eagle again, he flew into the sky, where he still lives. Since that time, Apache curers have had power from eagles. (In the Navajo versions, it is explicitly stated that the eagles rewarded the hero by giving him the Bead Chant, which he taught his people on returning to earth.)

As noted, this story, at least in the Navajo version, is theoretically a part of the Emergence cycle, whose far-flung branches encompass the entirety of Navajo mythology.

Emergence styles

The distinctive, pictorial style of the Bird Nester's song, with its shifting colors, belongs mainly to Navajo lore, though it also affects Jicarilla myths, as well as those of the Western Apache. In an older Navajo variant, the Emergence story starts at the very beginning with a characteristic litany of images that sets the scene in the Black World:

"It was named water everywhere, black world, one word [*sic*], and trees standing. It was also called white-shell waves moving, turquoise waves moving, white shell stands vertical, and turquoise stands vertical. Here where the sun would rise in the future, blackness rose up and whiteness rose up. There where blackness and whiteness rose together, First Man came into being."

Passages like this turn The Emergence into a visionary experience, in sharp contrast to the approach taken by Pueblo narrators, who see it as a kind of historical novel, reflecting familiar customs, even manners. In variants from Zuni pueblo, the story begins with polite exchanges between the underworld beings and the twin war gods, who have come to lead them upward:

"They came to the [lowest] world. It was black. The people could not see each other. They felt one another with their hands and recognized their faces. They said, 'Some stranger has come. Where is it that you have come from? It is our fathers, the bow priests [war gods].' They ran to feel them and they said, 'Our fathers, you have come. Teach us how to get out of this place. We have heard of our father Sun and we wish to see him.' The two answered, 'We have come to bring you to the other world where you can see him. Will you come with us?' The people answered, 'Yes, we wish to go.' "

Such polished manners recall the description of the Pueblos written in the 1930s by the Pueblo specialist Ruth Benedict, who found these people to be supremely cool, an "Apollonian" island surrounded by cultures in the grip of "Dionysian dogma." It was an invidious comparison, flattering the subject of Benedict's own studies. Gladys Reichard, another anthropologist of the period and a champion of Navajo artistry, countered by suggesting that Pueblos were uninspired. Generalizations of this nature, now discredited, were originally offered under the assumption that the people in question would not be reading what was written about them. That assumption, not valid then, would be unthinkable today.

Seven

Heroes and Their Grandmothers

Old Woman *Momoy*

The myths of the Chumash, whose now extinct culture once dominated the area northwest of Lost Angeles, were virtually unknown until the field notes of the late J. P. Harrington began to be sorted and analyzed in the 1970s. It is still too early to say whether Chumash mythology belongs more to the Southwest or to central California; possibly the latter. But by far the best-preserved narratives Harrington was able to obtain from the last Chumash speakers are six variants of a monster-ridding cycle, which conforms to the Southwest pattern of child heroes aided by a grandmother.

The old woman of the story is called *Momoy,* a Chumash word for the hallucinogenic drug toloache, made from datura, or jimsonweed. In one of the variants it is said that *Momoy* simply washed her hands in a bowl of water and gave it to her grandson to drink, so he would become "more courageous and manlike." Her uncanny ability to predict the dangers he would encounter —a standard motif in myths of this type—probably led to her identification with the drug.

In one of the stories the hero was the child of *Momoy*'s daughter, who was seduced by a bear, then eaten by him when he discovered she was pregnant. (A bear, it was said, cannot stand to see a pregnant woman without killing her.) After her daughter's death, *Momoy* searched the scene of the crime and found a spot of blood on an alder leaf. Crying, she took it home and covered it with a basket, and after a while it turned into a baby boy. As the child grew, *Momoy* made him progressively larger bows and arrows, until at last he was ready to set out on his monster-slaying adventures.

In a few of the variants there are twin heroes, and sometimes Coyote takes the place of *Momoy* as their wise helper. Among their adversaries are *Haphap,* the sucking monster (he inhales people with his powerful breath); a fiery ogress called the Burner; a murderous weasel; and the bear who killed *Momoy*'s daughter. After each adventure, the hero (or the heroes), typically returns to *Momoy,* who warns him of the next danger. In the end, however, he departs for a distant country or goes into the sky to live with the sun.

Flute Lure

The story of Flute Lure is the lesser of the two principal myths of the western half of the Southwest. (The other is the omnibus creation tale called The Dying God.) The heroes of Flute Lure share certain qualities with the typical Indian deliverer, yet their story is not a monster-ridding cycle in the obvious sense. Reminiscent of the subarctic Athapascan myths of death and sexuality, it is a story of dangerous females and how a hero finally gets rid of them.

In a Papago version of some complexity, twin boys are delivered to a woman who drags herself painfully through the mountains, singing:

> *Towering rocks*
> *sounding evening*
> *with them*
> *I am crying.*

After the children are born, and as they rapidly mature, she sends them to the eagle's nest to get feathers for arrows, shows them where to find wood for bows, then sings:

> *Bows now are made,*
> *Arrows now are made.*
> *Toward the west we will try them.*
> *You can watch them fly, my boys.*

Next she sends them to get canes for making flutes, and with their flute-playing the twins lure the two daughters of Buzzard. Promptly marrying the girls, they return with them to Buzzard's camp, where they are killed by his henchman, Blue Hawk, who sings: "Hanging motionless in the sky, yet terrible in its power to destroy."

But one of the girls is already pregnant. She gives birth to a hero who travels to his dead father's mother, obtains magic power from her, and returns to kill Buzzard, singing: "Who is the man who killed an enemy and has no joy?" Traveling again to the grandmother, he shows her the scalp and they exult together.

The grandmother now leaves for "another land" across the ocean, while the hero pays a last visit to his mother. Setting out to find the grandmother again, he is pursued by his mother and her sister, who sing:

Where am I running from, that I come here?
Am I a crazy woman with a painted face?

At the shore he lays his bow on the water, and it becomes a rainbow bridge across the ocean. As he reaches the far shore, and twists the bow, the pursuing women fall into the water, becoming shore birds. He rejoins the grandmother, and they live together from then on.

Spider Woman and the twins

In the Pueblo Emergence cycle, especially as told at Zuni, the twin war gods help the first beings ascend from the underworld, sometimes by planting herbs or trees that the people can climb. In a rare Hopi version the twins are the grandsons of Spider Woman, who herself plants the reed that penetrates the underworld sky.

The monster-ridding cycle with the grandmother as counselor is an entirely different story and one that is not taken as seriously by the Pueblos as it is by their neighbors. Older versions from Zia, Acoma, and a few other towns treat the theme with dignity. Yet for many Pueblo storytellers it has become a mere adventure tale, often with farcical elements, even though the main characters are Spider Woman and the sacred twins.

Considered to be war gods throughout the pueblos, the twins are also looked upon as little boys. At Zuni they are called the *Ahayúta.* In the Tewa pueblos they are the *Towa é* (little people). Among the Hopi, the elder of the two takes the name *Pohánghoya* or *Pókang,* and the pair are known in English as the Pokangs.

In a story collected recently, the Pokangs, after scaring their grandmother to death with a dead buzzard, laugh and dig her a grave on the side of a hill. When she unexpectedly comes to, they tie her hands, continue laughing, and roll her down the slope a few times before taking her back home.

In the eastern pueblos, myths and anecdotes about the war gods grade imperceptibly into a large class of stories that might be called fairy tales. Here, perhaps more than in any other area, we can speak of oral literature designed for children. Sometimes children themselves are the storytellers.

According to an old report from Taos, grandparents would assemble as many as twenty of their grandchildren for a winter's night of tale-telling, and each guest in turn would offer a story. As the audience grew sleepy, the stories became shorter. Toward daybreak, if someone were in the middle of too long a story, someone else would say, "Let's make him [the unending story-teller] *lamopolúna* (feces roll up)." Then they would tie him in a blanket, carry him out to the trash heap, and roll him down. If he could free himself and catch somebody, that one in turn would be rolled down the slope, and the others would all run back to the house.

Changing Woman

Navajo and Apache mythology assigns the usual grandmother role to the heroes' mother, who becomes a major figure in the religion of these tribes, particularly the Navajo. She is the goddess *Estsánatlehi* (changing woman), so called because of her power to grow old and become young again, like the earth as it passes from winter to summer.

Unlike most American Indian monster-ridding tales, the Navajo cycle is not an allegory whose significance has to be guessed. It is actually a doctrine, which spells out the origin of the monsters and connects their death to world salvation.

The sequence of events begins with The Separation of the Sexes, said by some to have occurred in the underworld, though others place it shortly after the emergence. In order to prove that the women could not live by themselves, the men abandoned them and went to live on the far side of a river. During the separation the women used sticks, cacti, and other objects to satisfy their sexual desire, with the result that they gave birth to monsters.

When these monsters, or "enemy gods," had terrorized the earth for some years, dangerously reducing the population, First

Man and First Woman discovered a baby girl in a rain cloud on top of a mountain. This was Changing Woman. Fed on pollen and dew, she grew rapidly, soon becoming eligible for her puberty ceremony. Afterward, she exposed her body to sunlight and dripping water and gave birth to the twin heroes *Nayénezgani* (monster slayer) and *Tobadjishtchíni* (child of the water).

The next part of the story, called The Two Came to Their Father, concerns the twins' journey to the Sun, who tests them to see if they can smoke his pipe and withstand the heat of a red-hot oven. When they do, he acknowledges them as his children and gives them magic weapons against the enemy gods. In these episodes, Spider Woman steps in temporarily with advice that enables the young heroes to meet their father's tests.

The boys now return to their mother, and the cycle continues with the epic known as Monsterway. First the twins kill the giant *Yéitso,* who carries people off in his pack basket. When they have brought his scalp home to Changing Woman, they hold a dance to celebrate the victory. Next comes The Attack on the Giant Elk (in which a burrowing animal leads the heroes to a spot directly beneath the monster's heart), followed by expeditions against the giant bird, the kicking monster, the looking monsters (who kill with a glance), and the cannibal bear. Then Changing Woman herself summons a storm that kills most of the remaining enemy gods, leaving only Old Age, Cold Woman, Poverty, Hunger, and a few others.

Their work finished, the twins retire to the north, and Changing Woman goes to live on an island at the far side of the western sea, where her consort, the Sun, can visit her at the end of each day. Surrounding her new home are four mountains, replicas of the sacred mountains that mark the boundaries of Navajo territory, east, south, west, and north. By dancing on each of these in turn, she produces rain clouds (east), fabrics and jewels (south), "plants of all kinds" (west), and corn and animals (north).

The story of Changing Woman, much embellished and with Monsterway deemphasized or omitted, accounts for the origin of the Navajo ritual complex called Blessingway. Performed for "good hope," Blessingway songs and procedures make up the childbirth rite, the girls' puberty rite, the wedding rite, and the house-blessing ceremony for a new home.

The Monsterway epic, on the other hand, gives rise to songs of exorcism, which can be fitted into the Navajo Night Chant and other healing ceremonials. For most Apache groups the monster-ridding epic was at one time the principal myth. Whereas some groups gave precedence to Monster Slayer, it was his brother, Child of the Water, who took the leading role in the story as told by the Chiricahua and Mescalero Apache, and for these tribes Child of the Water was the culture hero.

Among the Navajo, the lore of Changing Woman occupies the favored position. In the view of native ritualists, Blessingway, based on the myth of this rejuvenating goddess, "controls" the entire ceremonial system. That is, each ceremonial must include at least one Blessingway song in order to sanctify it—which lends support to the observation made repeatedly by outsiders that Changing Woman is the central deity of Navajo religion.

Eight

The Dying God

Toads and frogs

The idea of a myth age, when people were animals, is taken for granted by storytellers in the Southwest, just as it is along the Northwest Coast and in other regions. For the Pueblos and their immediate neighbors the prehuman condition existed in the underworld before the emergence. In some Zuni versions, for example, the people are said to have crawled like toads when they reached the earth's surface. The twin war gods made them human by cutting off their tails and horns and slitting their webbed hands to give them fingers.

Later, as the people began migrating toward the world's center, where they would build Zuni pueblo, some of their children turned into toads and lizards while crossing a shallow river. They sank back to the underworld, and these were the first deaths.

Whatever form it may take, the origin of death finds a place in nearly every well-developed Indian mythology, either prefiguring the human condition or actually accompanying the change from animal to human life. For the Takic and Yuman peoples of the western Southwest, it becomes the grand theme, climaxing the creation cycle, which serves as the basic myth for the funerals and mourning anniversaries that are the principal ceremonies in these tribes.

The agent of death is Frog, and his (or her) victim is the Creator and culture hero himself, the so-called dying god.

For the original natives of the Los Angeles area, the Gabrielino and Luiseño, the story began with the mating of the female earth and the male sky, said to have been sister and brother. From this union were born all the people of the myth age, including *Wiyót*, who was their leader. For reasons that varied from narrator to narrator, the sorcerer Frog plotted to kill *Wiyót*. According to some, it was simply a matter of arranging the first death. Others said *Wiyót* had become too harsh a leader, or that he had insulted Frog by thinking her skinny and she had read his thoughts.

Because of Frog's sorcery, *Wiyót* fell mortally ill. As soon as he was dead, the people gathered wood for a funeral pyre and held the first cremation. When the body had burned, all except the heart, Coyote broke through the crowd of spectators, seized the heart, and ate it. Afterward, *Wiyót* rose up as the moon, whose regular reappearance was taken as a sign of continuing life.

At Luiseño funerals in the old days, a ritualist would cut a piece from the back or shoulder of the corpse and eat it, or pretend to eat it, in full view of the mourners. This was said to commemorate Coyote's theft of the culture hero's heart.

Brother gods

Yuman versions of the Dying God story also begin with the mating of Mother Earth and Father Sky—one of the characteristic motifs of Southwest lore. But here the pair gives birth to two creator gods, not one. According to the Diegueño—the westernmost of the Yuman groups—the parents were earth and water, whom the newborn brothers separated by pushing the water upward to form the sky.

As told by the Mojave, the story opens with the mutual touching of earth and sky somewhere far to the west, which results in the birth of all creatures, including *Matavílya* and his younger brother, *Mastamhó.* By stretching his arms, *Matavílya* locates the center of the earth, leads the people to that spot in four great strides, and establishes the first house. There he offends his daughter, Frog, by making what is interpreted as an indecent overture (though *Matavílya* does not mean it in that way). To punish him, Frog gains control over his body by swallowing his excrement, bewitching him so that he falls sick and dies. Then follows the familiar episode of the first cremation and the theft of the god's heart by Coyote.

After his brother's death, *Mastamhó* leads the people to the extreme north, again in four strides, and punctures the earth with his "cane of breath and spittle," causing the Colorado River to gush forth. Eventually the waters reach flood stage, but *Mastamhó* puts the people on his arms and carries them safely to the mountain *Avikwamé* (Newberry Mountain, north of the town of Needles, California).

On the mountain he gives future shamans their dream power while they stand before him either as unborn children or as little boys. Afterward, he teaches the Mojave to farm, to cook, to speak, and to count, then changes into a fish eagle and flies off "without power of recollection, ignorant and infested with vermin."

Reasoning that the brother gods had ceased to be divine, the Mojave did not address them in prayer. Yet all Mojave shamans believed that as children they had stood on the mountain with *Mastamhó.* As for *Matavílya,* his death set the pattern for the all-important Mojave cremation ceremonies, which have continued into modern times.

Like the Mojave, the inland Takic recognize two major deities, usually said to be brothers, sometimes father and son. In either case, both are dying gods. One, in a foul mood, sinks into the underworld after creating an ill-formed race that he had hoped would become human. The other creates normal humans, but succumbs to the sorcery of Frog, dies, and is cremated in the usual fashion.

As with most other Southwest tribes (the western Pueblos excepted), the inland Takic have a strong tradition of punctuating a myth with songs. For ceremonial purposes, the songs that belong to The Dying God may be sung as a series without the interconnecting narrative. To perform them is to "sing the creation story," and this is still being done at Takic funerals on reservations southeast of Los Angeles.

Elder Brother

Compared with their neighbors to the west, the Piman tribes of southern Arizona pay little attention to death, preferring private burial over public cremation. In their view, the ceremonial telling of the creation story belonged not to funerals but to the winter solstice, at which time the myth was recited in a four-day session. Folkloristically, however, the story is much the same as The Dying God of the Yumans and the Takic, to which the Pimans add an emergence motif, perhaps borrowed from the Pueblos.

In the beginning, according to these tribes, Earthmaker created the sky and the earth, and the two touched, giving birth to a second deity, called Elder Brother. Some versions have Buzzard and Coyote assisting in the acts of creation, and in one variant Coyote steals the corpse's heart after the first death (of a mortal, not a god). In other accounts there are no deaths until the world flood, caused by the tears of an abandoned baby.

Following the flood, which killed all the first mortals, Earthmaker and Elder Brother each made people out of clay. But

Earthmaker's clay figures were misshapen, and after arguing with Elder Brother he sank into the earth. Elder Brother's creations were the *Hohokám* (an advanced town-dwelling culture that vanished about A.D. 1450). All went well until their creator molested some of the maidens during the girls' puberty ceremony. In retaliation the people killed Elder Brother, or, as in some versions, the sorcerer Buzzard shot him dead with sunrays.

After four years, however, Elder Brother revived and followed the setting sun into the underworld. From there he led an emergence of new people, the present Pimans, as an army against the *Hohokám.* When the *Hohokám* had been driven away, Elder Brother created deer for the Pimans to hunt, instituted the winter solstice festival, and finally retired to the underworld.

As the dying god who returned leading an army, Elder Brother was the natural patron of the war rite, performed before going on a raid. To open the ceremony, an orator recited one of the typical Piman mystery speeches describing the journey of a hero in quest of supernatural power. In this case the hero was Elder Brother as he followed the sun's route across the sky and into the underworld prior to his reappearance as war leader.

Identifying with Elder Brother, the warriors were strengthened for their mission—though not without risk. According to the Piman theory of disease, a person who falls ill may be diagnosed as having contracted the special sickness connected with a rite in which he has participated. If it is "enemy consequence" sickness, the cure is to re-recite the Elder Brother speech in order to rechannel the ceremonial power gone awry.

The Piman war rite was last held in the 1950s and perhaps will not be held again. But "enemy consequence" sickness cannot be declared extinct so long as anyone who participated in that ceremony is still alive.

Ultimate origins

The tribes of the western Southwest do not always trace their culture heroes to the mating of earth and sky. In a version from

Cahuilla, one of the inland Takic languages, the twin heroes are born in tiny cocoons that result from the clashing of red lightning and white lightning in the primal void. In Piman versions, one of the two creators existed before the appearance of earth and sky, as we have seen, and in one particularly elegant variant it is said that this first creator was preceded by darkness, which gathered itself into a great mass. Inside it developed the spirit of the deity, who drifted to and fro like a "fluffy wisp of cotton."

For the Luiseño, sky and earth were the ultimate originators. However, according to native theorists active around the turn of the century, this pair was not always as it is now, having developed from nothingness in a series of mystical transitions. At first there were Vacant and Empty, which became Pale White and Not Alive Not Being, which in turn were changed into Upheaval and Falling Downward, which at last became Night (the sky) and Earth.

A variant has it that the first being was called Vacant Empty, who existed through eight time periods named not-alive-not-being, upheaval, falling downward, working in darkness, working together deep down, pale white, dimness of twilight, and, finally, a period of cessation called things at a standstill. Then Vacant Empty created Sky and Earth, and the two "became conscious of each other."

These highly unusual versions make mention of a new deity called *Chingíchngish,* who in one of the stories completely replaces *Wiyót,* the traditional Luiseño culture hero. According to the revised story, *Chingíchngish* was born of Earth, who immediately had to hide him because he terrified her other children. She taught them to worship him, however, and if they failed to obey his stern moral code they were bitten or stung by the "avengers," rattlesnake, bear, scorpion, rosebush, and others.

The worship of *Chingíchngish* is thought to have arisen among the Gabrielino during the early mission period (1771–1833), perhaps in an attempt to block the inroads of Christianity. Although it spread as far south as the Diegueño, its greatest success was with the Luiseño, midway between Los Angeles and San Diego. Today the *Chingíchngish* religion still has a few Luiseño adherents on the small Rincon and Pauma reservations in northern San Diego County.

Montezuma

Less clearly defined than *Chingíchngish* is the heroic, sometimes Christlike figure found in revisionist myths of Arizona and New Mexico under the native name *Pósayamo* or the imported title "Montezuma." These stories range from the mythic to the legendary, occasionally borrowing from the Christian Gospels and from the history of the Spanish conquest of Mexico.

During the nineteenth century there was a well-developed cult of Montezuma in the eastern pueblos, where sacred fires were kept burning in his honor, awaiting the day when he would come to deliver the people from non-Indian intruders. As explained in a Tewa story, the hero was born to a virgin who had become pregnant by swallowing piñon nuts. Though as a child he was treated as an outcast, he had a spirit father who spoke to him, predicting that he would one day "rule all the Indians." "That Montezuma went south," commented the storyteller. But when he returns, all Mexicans and Anglos will leave, and "that will be our rich time."

Formerly the Piman tribes told a version of the creation tale in which the dying god was not Elder Brother but Montezuma. After leading the Pimans to the earth's surface and defeating the race that had killed him, he went south into Mexico. Elder Brother, it will be remembered, retired to the underworld.

A subtler adaptation is preserved in nineteenth-century Zuni variants of The Emergence, which have it that the first being to reach the surface was the "foremost of men," the sacred *Póshayanki* (Zuni form of *Pósayamo*). Pitying the people in the underworld, this hero found his way into the light and acted as interces-

Posayamo Calling the Food Animals, watercolor by Richard Martinez, San Ildefonso. Museum of Fine Arts, Houston.

sor with the Sun father, asking him to deliver the people from darkness. In response, the Sun created the twin war gods, who led the people up.

Recent Zuni versions have omitted the intercessor, and in general the native people of the Southwest have come to rely less and less on myths that are not traditional. A purifying cult like the *Chingíchngish* religion or a messianic myth of Montezuma-*Pósayamo* is not needed in an era when political action and lawsuits provide an obviously more effective means of dealing with outsiders.

In fact, by telling the old myths straight, Indians demonstrate that they are in touch with their roots, which impresses courts and lawmakers. In the 1970s the Mashpee of Massachusetts failed in their bid for land rights on Cape Cod because, for one reason, they had insufficient traditions to show that they were a separate people. For the typical tribe of the Southwest this would hardly have been a problem, though it can be pointed out that there are a few, like the tiny Chumash remnant, who must now try to regain their old lore by reading books, and others, like the Gabrielino, who are remembered only as a lost branch on the American family tree.

Part Four ↘

WEST
CENTRAL

Nine

Creators of California

"The sun stood still"

As used here, the name California applies only to about two
thirds of the state, stretching from the northeast corner to a
cut-off line two hundred miles south of San Francisco. Before the
Gold Rush of 1849 this was a region of village dwellers, who did
not farm, who seldom traveled, and who almost never made war.
The hunting and the fishing were good and the edible acorns so
abundant that the region supported a population denser than
most areas where farming was practiced.

   Though people were blessed with leisure, artistic accomplishments remained modest—except for two features: the mainly female art of basket weaving, as refined as any in the world, and the mostly male art of mythmaking, noted for inventive tales of world creation. Today, basketry is still a vital if small industry. But mythmaking, a far more fragile craft, had all but ceased by the 1930s and is not likely to be revived.

The extent to which it was a living art, as late as the 1920s, can be judged by this passage from the Pomo mythmaker W. Ralganal Benson. To grasp its full significance requires a moment's thought: "He walked over the hill. On the other side it was dark, he sat down, there was no light. He went on. Up in the sky there was light. Then he rolled the earth over, it turned over, he pushed it over. 'This is the way you will perform,' said *Madúmda,* 'now it is dark, and now it is light, and now it is sunlight.' Now it is performed."

The idea is similarly expressed in an Achomawi myth composed about the same time. "Then the old man reached down and drew out something from under him and shook it over the east, and threw it to the west. The ground shook, the world began turning over, the moon drifted, the sun stood still."

These are stories that account for the earth's rotation, a theme not found outside California, nor within that region, to be sure, prior to the modern period. But even if new, such speculation stems from a strong and no doubt old tradition of poetic reasoning about the origin of the world.

The council of animals

As a whole, the mythology of California focuses on origination rather than deliverance, with supernatural animals of the myth age taking turns or cooperating in the various acts of creation. World floods and world fires are the characteristic turning points, providing opportunities for starting the process all over again. Finally, with or without help from a transformer, the animal people change into the animals of today, and the myth age comes to a close.

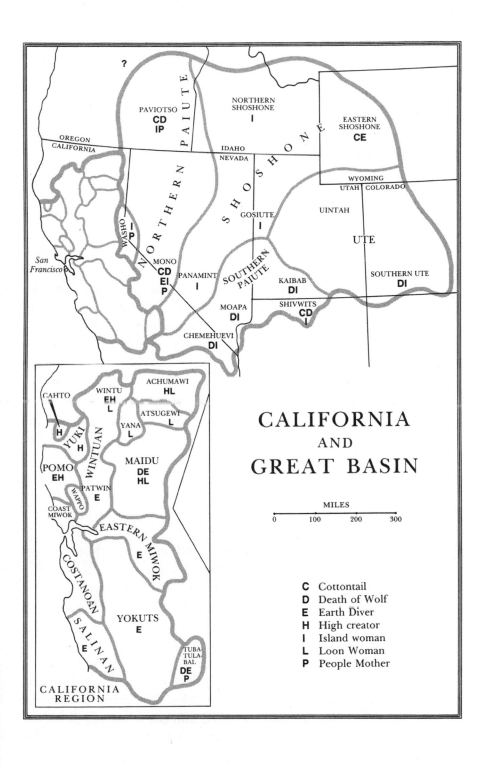

?

PAVIOTSO
**CD
IP**

NORTHERN
SHOSHONE
I

EASTERN
SHOSHONE
CE

OREGON
CALIFORNIA

NORTHERN   PAIUTE

S H O S H O N E

IDAHO
NEVADA

WYOMING
UTAH   COLORADO

WASHO
**I
P**

GOSIUTE
I

UINTAH

UTE

San
Francisco

MONO
**CD
EI
P**

PANAMINT
I

SOUTHERN
PAIUTE

KAIBAB
DI

SOUTHERN UTE
DI

MOAPA
DI

SHIVWITS
**CD
I**

CHEMEHUEVI
DI

CALIFORNIA
AND
GREAT BASIN

MILES

| 0 | 100 | 200 | 300 |

ACHUMAWI
HL

CAHTO

WINTU
**EH
L**

ATSUGEWI
L

YUKI
H

YANA
L

POMO
EH

WINTUAN

MAIDU
**DE
HL**

WAPPO

PATWIN
E

COAST
MIWOK

EASTERN MIWOK

COSTANOAN

E

SALINAN
E

YOKUTS
E

TUBA-
TULA-
BAL
**DE
P**

CALIFORNIA
REGION

C Cottontail
D Death of Wolf
E Earth Diver
H High creator
I Island woman
L Loon Woman
P People Mother

In the lore of the southern tribes, it is possible to see that the mythic animals are ancestral figures, since Eagle, Coyote, Hawk, Fox, and the others are clan names as well as the names of creators. In the south, Eagle is often the chief, with Coyote playing an important role either as helper or as adversary. Moving north, we find Coyote merging with the figure of an anthropomorphic creator, who eventually loses his animal nature, at least in the eyes of the more sophisticated mythmakers. Even here, however, the lesser aspects of the creation are assigned to the animal powers, and Coyote reappears as his old self.

Local and individual variation make for a patchwork of myths, many of which appear to be unique. In a Coast Miwok story the earth is revealed when Coyote shakes his blanket over the primeval waters, causing them to dry up. In a Wappo myth, after Chicken Hawk has complained to Coyote that the first people don't talk, Coyote goes to Old Man Moon and comes back with a bag of words. It would be hard if not impossible to find duplicates of these particular stories. But there are others that have circulated widely enough to be called typical:

Earth Diver. This is the well-known story found east of the Rockies and in the subarctic Athapascan region. In California, the one who brings up mud to form the earth is usually the turtle or the duck.

Humans from sticks. Coyote puts sticks in a sweathouse and says, "Well, may these become people!" and they do. In some versions, feathers are substituted for sticks.

Lizard hand. Coyote, who has a closed fist, wanted us to have hands like his. But Lizard said, "No, they must have my hand." Since Lizard won the argument, we have an open hand with five fingers.

Origin of death. Wolf said, "Coyote, the human being must have two deaths. That will be our rule." But Coyote said, "What is the use of two deaths? When a person dies, we have to cry. The tears must dry on our cheeks." This argument, of course, was won by Coyote.

Though less important than creation tales, monster-ridding cycles are by no means lacking. In a minor epic of the Salinan, the heroes Hawk and Raven kill a double-headed serpent, a skunk, a one-footed cannibal, and a boulder who throws people to a flock of little flesh-eating birds. The Eastern Miwok once had a similar cycle, with Coyote and Prairie Falcon as the heroes. Among the Costanoan, the monster slayer was Duck Hawk.

The *utentbe* style

How did these stories sound in performance? In the circular earth lodges of the Eastern Miwok they were sometimes chanted, usually by a professional myth teller, or *utentbe,* who made the rounds of the villages, taking payment in baskets and other valuables.

The myths were told at night, the only acceptable time for reciting stories, and as smoke from the fire rose to the hole in the center of the heavy-beamed roof, the *utentbe* might begin by explaining how the animal people got ready for the world flood:

"Prairie Falcon told his people to prepare. He said, 'Get ready, Eagle. Get ready, Flicker. Get ready, Dove. Get ready, Woodpecker. Get ready, Quail. Get ready, Kingbird. Get ready, Hummingbird. We are going. We are going. We are going, going toward the north. Hurry, prepare, for we must go at once, must go at once, must go at once.' So he said, when he told his people to prepare. 'We shall take the people. We shall take the people to the place where my father always goes.'

"Prairie Falcon said to Eagle, 'Tell everyone, Eagle. Tell everyone, Eagle. Have your people prepare. Tell California Jay to come. Tell Coyote to come. Tell Hummingbird to come. We will go to the top of the great mountain.' "

At such a leisurely pace, it is understandable that sessions with the *utentbe* often lasted the night. This was customary throughout the region. Among the Pomo, as the night wore on, each story ended with the obligatory prayer, "From the east and from the west may the mallard girls hurry and bring the morning."

Loon Woman

A favorite of the northern tribes was the myth of Loon Woman, who was said by some myth tellers to have been responsible for the world fire. As the story opens, she stands at the edge of a pool, fascinated by the sight of a long hair floating on the surface.

"She saw a hair, she took it up, looked at it, looked at the hair, one hair, she looked at the hair she had found. 'Whose hair? I want to know.' She looked at it long, looked at the hair, one long hair. The woman thought, 'Whose hair?' she thought." (Notice the repetitive *utentbe*-like style in this passage from a Wintu variant.)

Returning home with her find, she compared it to the hair on her eldest brother's head and fell hopelessly in love with him. Without revealing her secret, she arranged to have this brother accompany her on a camping trip, and during the first night she crept next to him where he lay sleeping and wrapped her arms around his body.

The brother woke first, appalled that he was lying in his sister's embrace. Careful not to wake her, he freed himself and put a rotten log in his place. Then he ran home, bringing the awful news. To escape the horror, everybody jumped into a basket that was supposed to carry them to the sky, warning each other not to look down or the basket would fall.

By this time the sister had awakened. She rushed home, saw the rising basket, and in a fury set fire to the family's lodge (or to the whole world, according to some). While the basket was still rising, Coyote peeped over the edge. The basket fell, and the family was burned to death in the flames. When the ashes had cooled, the sister gathered up the victims' blackened hearts in order to wear them as a necklace—and from this comes the black neckband of the common loon.

Notice that Coyote seems to be a member of the family. In the

---

When Coyote Leaves the Res, acrylic, 1980, by Harry Fonseca, Maidu. Heard Museum, Phoenix.

words of an Achomawi storyteller, humans in the full sense of the word were not created until after the world had been spoiled by that "crazy woman, Loon."

High creators

A generation after the initial shock of the Gold Rush, revitalistic cults began sweeping through the northern California tribes, first the Ghost Dance of 1870, then the Earth Lodge and the Bole-Maru, or Dreamer, religions. These movements, which stressed change and gave authority to personal inspiration at the expense of received wisdom, evidently paved the way for a new era in mythmaking.

Norelputus of the Wintu, the most celebrated of the new myth-opoets, is known to have been active in the post-Gold Rush religions. Not without the support of his tribesmen, he composed myths that departed from the standard tribal lore, creating an elaborate mythology centering around the high god *Ólelbis* (one who is above) and his consort *Mem Loimis* (water woman).

Among the Achomawi, the folklorist C. Hart Merriam found myths of similar quality, chronicling the activities of the deity World's Heart. World's Heart lived in the center of the earth, unlike *Ólelbis,* whose lodge was at the top of the sky. Similarly, the Pomo god *Madúmda* is said to have dwelled in a radiant white house in the lower of two upper worlds. *Madúmda* and World's Heart are the two deities given credit, quite independently, for having initiated the earth's rotation.

But influences traceable to either Christianity or modern science are not really typical of these latter-day mythologies. For the most part they incorporate Indian ideas, and the high creator concept itself has deep native roots. Long before the Gold Rush, the now virtually extinct Yuki were reciting myths of *Taikómol* (solitude walker), the creator who began as a voice in the sea foam, then sprang up in human form and established the earth by superimposing a cross on the surface of the water. Young men learned the complete creation cycle at a *"Taikómol* school," held during the winter months. In these sessions the god was impersonated by a masked dancer, who also appeared in medicinal rites.

The entire complex of god-impersonating rituals, extending from the Yuki and the Pomo on the west to the Maidu on the east, has been labeled the Kuksu cult, and it is more or less within the territory of this undoubtedly old religion that myths of the anthropomorphic creator were developed.

Among the Cahto, close neighbors of the Yuki, the god was called *Nágaicho* (great walker). When the horned earth monster rose out of the water, Great Walker simply spread clay between its eyes, added reeds, brush, and trees, and said, "I have finished." In the case of the Maidu Earth Namer, it seems there was a bird's nest—some said a robin's nest—floating on the water. The creator trussed it with ropes and stretched it in all directions until it became the dry land. But the story varied considerably from teller to teller. In some versions the bird itself was said to have made the earth.

In many of these myths the creator is hindered by Coyote. Or he may be assisted by an even higher deity, in which case the creator sometimes betrays trickster tendencies that suggest a Coyote-like personality on *his* part.

Non-Indians are quicker to see God in an anthropomorphic earth maker than in a coyote or a bird man. But in so doing they fail to appreciate a widespread Indian point of view. An Achomawi, well versed in the myths of his tribe, once asked, "What is this thing that the white people call God? They are always talking about it. It's goddam this and goddam that, and in the name of the god, and the god made the world. Who is that god? They say that Coyote is the Indian God, but if I say to them that God is Coyote, they get mad at me. Why?"

Ten ↘

Great Basin Heroes and Heroines

Cottontail

Living was difficult in the dry open country of the Great Basin. Lacking the acorn crops that enriched the Californians, the Basin people foraged for roots, bulbs, and greens, rounding out their diet with small game. Settlements, if such they can be called, often amounted to no more than the brush shelter of a single family, with no neighbors in sight.

People did get together for communal hunts or an occasional pine nut harvest, and these events afforded opportunities for exchanging stories. So far as is known, myths were told primarily for entertainment. There were few or no connections with religion or with social institutions. It has been said that the Basin taboo against eating coyotes grew out of the local mythology, in which Coyote is a major figure. But this rather slight association between myth and custom may be no more than coincidence.

A similar argument, in reverse, has been made on behalf of the rabbit, who is thought to have been a hero in myths of the western Great Lakes area because rabbits are an important item in the diet. Whether the conjecture is true or not, it is interesting to note that the cottontail of Basin diets also plays a part in Basin myths —though his role is a decidedly ambiguous one.

With the figure of the rogue Cottontail, we are introduced at once to the shadowy side of the Basin myth teller, whose vision seems to come from inner drives and impulses. Rather than supplying obvious answers, this is a mythology that follows byways and takes sudden turns.

Basically, Cottontail is the story of an adventurer of the myth age who made war on the sun, either to reduce its excessive warmth or to redirect it in a higher course. In a Paviotso version, Cottontail himself is a hunter of cottontail rabbits, disgusted because the sun cuts short the hunt by hiding behind mountains. Plotting revenge against the sun, he sets out across the earth, soon arriving at the home of North Wind, whose daughter he seduces. When her brothers complain, he burns them alive, then throws North Wind's daughter into the fire as well.

Continuing his journey, he meets Buzzard, who tries to press a thumb into his brain. Averting the danger, he retaliates by pressing a thumb into Buzzard's son's brain and by killing Buzzard himself with an arrow to the heart.

After further exploits in this vein, he falls in with another cottontail, said to be his brother. Together the two reach the end of the earth and watch as the sun rises out of the ocean and dries itself on a rock like an otter. Dry at last, it begins its ascent. But the brothers promptly shoot it down and cut out its gall, which they throw into the sky straight overhead, crying, "When you travel, do not go along the ridge of the mountains, but travel straight across the sky, so that we will have time to hunt."

Cottontail, whose worthy deeds seem outweighed by his brutality, belongs to a class of heroes that includes the brothers *Haínanu* and *Pamákasu* of the Paviotso and the Mono, also the Weasel brothers of the Shoshone. Were they to be offered up for our judgment, they would have to be pronounced among the meanest characters in Indian mythology.

The death of Wolf

The most persistent figure in Basin stories is the trickster-creator Coyote, sometimes called *Sinav* or *Sináwavi* in southern and eastern parts of the region. In company with his elder brother, usually Wolf, Coyote creates the earth by pouring sand on the primeval waters, creates light, steals fire, steals pine nuts, and releases impounded game animals. To tell them briefly, Coyote's exploits sound straightforward enough, but these incidents are typically embedded in complex myths that no two people would interpret in the same manner.

An impressive example is the episodic story that reaches its climax in the death of Wolf. In a Paviotso version it opens with The Theft of Pine Nuts, and the narrator starts right off with the mysterious statement "Coyote smelled pine nuts in the east, and blood gushed from his nose." After Coyote and Wolf have journeyed eastward and stolen the pine nuts, the pine nut owners pursue them, and in the attack Wolf is killed.

According to a different Paviotso narrator, the cycle begins with The Release of Impounded Game. Coyote sets the animals free, but in his efforts to keep the game for the exclusive use of his own people, he and Wolf are drawn into a war with an enemy tribe, and Wolf is killed. In a Shivwits variant, the war is with bear people, offended because Coyote has seduced and murdered a bear woman. Again Wolf is killed.

Oddly, Wolf loses his life because Coyote betrays him to the enemy. Yet, on account of Wolf's death, Coyote weeps inconsolably. In one version he cries for so many days that he becomes thin. When he goes to retrieve Wolf's hide, which the enemy is dishonoring, he is still in tears but excuses himself by saying that the smoke from the enemy's fire makes his eyes water.

Back home, he prepares to resuscitate the hide, but in his fumbling he unties the bag of darkness and cries aloud once more. Then he creates the light by shooting a red woodpecker feather into the air. At last he places the hide in damp sand (or under an anthill), and Wolf is restored.

In one of the Paviotso versions, the final scene is a discussion between Wolf and Coyote about whether humans will be immortal. In the more uninhibited Shivwits variant, Coyote repays himself for his trouble by sleeping with Wolf's wife.

As told by the Chemehuevi, the entire cycle was reminiscent of The Dying God of the Mojave and other Yuman tribes of the Southwest. The Chemehuevi even used it to explain the origin of their cremation and mourning ceremonies. Such a connection between myth and religion, so alien to the Basin, can be explained only by the presence of strong Mojave influence.

The island woman

One of the most striking incidents in the numerous recorded tales of Wolf and Coyote is the motif of the human race spilled from a jug. Coyote, or, less often, Wolf, puts seeds in a wickerwork jug, or bottle, and pours them out as human beings. Often the incident was included in an episodic creation myth built around the figure of a woman who lived on an island with her mother. In those days there were no tribes and few if any men to father them.

To find a man, the mother sends the daughter out over the earth—the newly formed earth, according to a Moapa version in which the mother herself is the earth maker. After several unsuccessful searches, the daughter returns with Coyote, who becomes her husband.

However, as he lies with her, Coyote discovers that his wife has a toothed vagina (the *vagina dentata* motif of folklorists, found throughout North America, as well as in Asia and in South America). To save himself, Coyote disarms the woman with a blunt instrument, usually a stick of wood.

After they have lived together for virtually no time at all, the wife gives birth to myriad tiny babies, which she drops into a jug. When the jug is full, she hands it to Coyote, ordering him to distribute its contents over the land.

If, for example, the story is told by a Panamint, it will be said that Coyote poured this tribe last, when the jug was nearly empty; therefore the Panamint are few. According to a Gosiute narrator, the last man to come out of the jug was covered with dust and tougher than all the others; he was the Gosiute.

People Mother

Another story about the prospective mother of tribes, and how she searched for a husband, was told by narrators along the western edge of the Basin. According to a Paviotso storyteller of the 1920s (when many of the published Basin myths were recorded), the heroine of the tale was a menstruant and therefore in seclusion when the other members of her household came under sudden attack. The assailant was a looking monster, whose fiery red gaze instantly killed all the people in the house, except for a sleeping child.

Wrapping the child in her blanket, the heroine fled. But when she made camp, the child was stolen and killed by a giant, who hung the little boy from his belt like a dead rabbit. Fleeing the giant, the woman found temporary safety at the home of Gopher Woman, where she gathered seeds and ground them.

As soon as she had a good supply of meal, she continued her journey, escaping a murderous flying head with the assistance of Woodrat, who hid her in his cave. Again traveling, she picked up the little boy, now revived, who had been killed by the giant, and together they reached the mountaintop home of the gentle hunter who would become the woman's husband.

The couple did not lie together at first, but drew their beds a little closer each night. Soon the woman began bearing children and in this way became People Mother, the mother of tribes.

The essence of myth

These Basin stories, even if stripped of all references to firsts and origins and even if we were not told that the characters lived in the old time, would still have the disjointed, kaleidoscopic quality that separates certain kinds of myth from normal, straightforward storytelling. The question is whether the seemingly jumbled incidents are accidental—the result of clumsiness on the part of the storyteller—or whether they are flashing the signals of a hidden message. The science of mythology rests on the latter assumption.

It was Franz Boas who dealt this uncertain science the near death blow from which it has never fully recovered. Disenchanted with nineteenth-century theories that linked myth to the rhythms of nature, Boas produced exhaustive reports, primarily on Northwest Coast and Eskimo myths, suggesting that the traditional tales were not subtle allegories of the coming and going of the seasons or of the movements of heavenly bodies, as many investigators had thought, but merely a kind of primitive fiction, depicting human situations.

Following Boas' lead, the anthropologist Julian H. Steward, in a critical essay on Basin mythology, used European literary standards to evaluate the various tales, concluding that many of the narrators had not perfected their art. Unrealistic elements were dismissed as "incoherent" or "entirely irrelevant." Criticizing the myth of the island woman, Steward found the dropping of the tiny babies into the jug to be "insufficiently motivated."

Boas himself was seldom so critical, at least in his published reports. But in his private writings he went further, noting in a letter dated October 3, 1883, "Then I went to the Bella Coolas, who told me another idiotic story. . . . The fact that I obtain these stories is interesting, but the stories themselves are more horrible than some of the Eskimo stories."

After Boas' initial thrusts, new ideas from continental Europe helped mythology regain a small measure of the status it was rapidly losing. Freudian dream theory inspired a few writers to see myth as a symbolic language for describing psychological problems. According to these theorists, myths concealed desires that were forbidden by normal society. Freud's early collaborator, Carl Jung, developed a somewhat more detailed—and more optimistic—approach, finding that problems dealt with in mythology were conflicts between opposing drives. As the story unfolded, these conflicts were neutralized in a symbolic healing process that promoted wholeness. Philosophers of the structuralist school adopted a similar view, though without the cheerful overtones. For them the pairs of conflicts, or opposites, were the given terms of an underlying intellectual problem, which the mythmaker tried to solve.

We may now take another look at the puzzling little boy in the myth of People Mother and wonder how he suddenly revived and why he was dragged back into the story near the end, only to be forgotten again. A Jungian view would be to take the boy as a male symbol that merges with the heroine to give her universality or wholeness. As a structuralist solution, it might be proposed that the boy stands for youth, which balances the heroine's maturity, offering a hidden resolution to the conflict over whether or not to marry.

But even within the confines of Jungianism or structuralism such interpretations would be tentative. They are, after all, only a means of groping for the native view of myth, which embraces variation and comprehends its rightness. As Steward, without objection, wrote in his study of Basin myths, the people who told these stories, fantastic as they might appear to outsiders, regarded them as "Gospel truth."

Part Five ↳

COAST-PLATEAU

Eleven ↘

Remaking the World

"Banishing evil,
helping the needy"

The watershed of the Columbia and the numerous short rivers
immediately to its north and south form a region of coastal valleys
and interior highlands that once shared a mythology of traveling
heroes. In this country the idea of an as-if-human age, or myth
time, everywhere present in North America, was perhaps more
insistent than in any other region.

As they progressed up or down the rivers, the heroes would
alert everybody, "The people are coming," or "A new generation

is on its way." As elsewhere, the ambiguous citizenry of the myth time were mostly animals that acted like people. Sometimes they were plants or even inanimate objects such as combs and awls. A story might begin, "A boy lived with his grandmother," but it was not to be assumed that these characters were human. The true humans were yet to come.

Along the lower reaches of the Klamath River in the northwest corner of California, a few tribes developed the concept of an age of immortals. The ancient ones were called *woge* by the Yurok, *ikaréya* by the Karok, and *kihúnai* by the Hupa. Evidently these beings were human, though the demigods who traveled the Klamath would no doubt have reminded some of the interior tribes of their own hero, Coyote.

The typical culture hero of the northern and western portions of this Coast-Plateau region was the Transformer, also known in Northwest Coast and Athapascan lore. Man-eating giants and, on the coast at least, ogresses who carried people off in their pack baskets haunted the world that the Transformer attempted to improve. More than a monster slayer, he had a hand in shaping the country's wealth, which, on a more modest scale than along the Northwest Coast, came principally from salmon and other fish. Roots and bulbs were also important and, especially in the east, big game.

Another, similar hero, best called the Trickster-Transformer, occupied a noticeable, if secondary, place, becoming dominant southward and eastward. Usually this figure was Coyote, and among the Sahaptian tribes of the southeastern part of the region he reigned unchallenged.

The differences between the two kinds of hero—the Transformer and the Trickster-Transformer—are less clear than in the case of Raven and the Northwest Coast Transformer called *Kánekelak, Kwehetí,* or *Hals.* In the Coast-Plateau region their adventures often overlap. They may even appear together in the same myth. Nevertheless, native attitudes toward the two remain fairly distinct.

Speaking of the Trickster-Transformer, a Chinook narrator could say, "Coyote continued his travels, sometimes doing right,

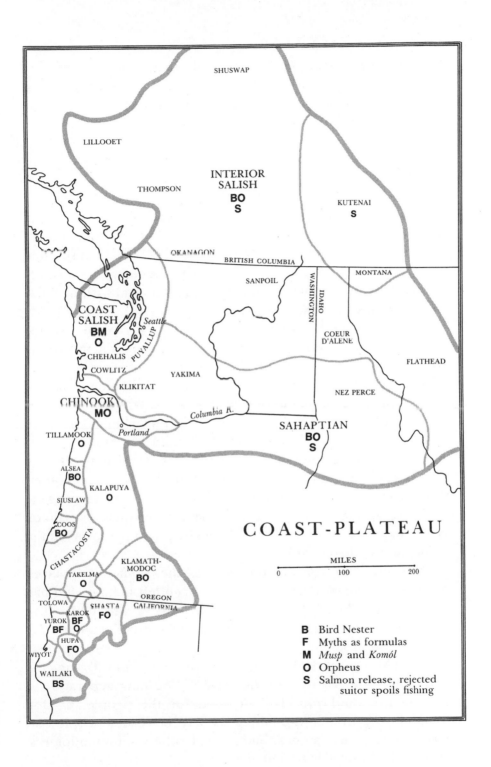

SHUSWAP

LILLOOET

THOMPSON

INTERIOR
SALISH
BO
S

KUTENAI
S

OKANAGON

BRITISH COLUMBIA

SANPOIL

MONTANA

COAST
SALISH
BM
O

Seattle

CHEHALIS

COWLITZ

PUYALLUP

WASHINGTON

IDAHO

COEUR
D'ALENE

FLATHEAD

KLIKITAT

YAKIMA

CHINOOK
MO

Columbia R.

NEZ PERCE

TILLAMOOK
O

Portland

SAHAPTIAN
BO
S

ALSEA
BO

KALAPUYA
O

SIUSLAW

COOS
BO

CHASTACOSTA

KLAMATH-
MODOC
BO

COAST-PLATEAU

TAKELMA
O

MILES

0   100   200

TOLOWA

OREGON
CALIFORNIA

KAROK **BF**

SHASTA
FO

YUROK **BF**

HUPA
FO

WIYOT

WAILAKI
BS

B Bird Nester
F Myths as formulas
M *Musp* and *Komól*
O Orpheus
S Salmon release, rejected
    suitor spoils fishing

at other times making mistakes, and all things good or bad were made so by him." More idealistic, the Salish Transformer Moon was said to "beautify" the earth, "banishing evil, helping the needy, and teaching the ignorant."

Moon

Storytellers among the southern Coast Salish sometimes began the Moon epic with an adaptation of The Star Husband, one of the most popular Indian folktales, found in every region south of the Arctic. The cycle therefore began with the story of two sisters sleeping out in the open, gazing up at the stars and wishing those bright bodies were their husbands.

The next thing they knew, they were in the sky world, married to two star men. With time, a baby was born. But the young women were dissatisfied with their new life, and when they accidentally punched a hole through the sky while digging roots and saw the earth far below, they began making a ladder out of twisted cedar boughs. As soon as it was finished, they climbed down to earth, taking the baby with them. This child was Moon.

After rejoining their people, the sisters decided to use the hanging ladder as a swing. While they played, their grandmother, Toad, took care of Moon. But Toad was blind, and as she sang to the baby, Dog Salmon stole him, carrying him off to the salmon country at the edge of the world. There he grew up, took a salmon bride, and had sons of his own.

Meanwhile, to console themselves, the women had taken Moon's cedar-bark diaper, which had been left behind, and had magically produced a second child by rinsing this diaper five times in water. They had also sent Bluejay, though without avail, to fetch Moon home.

At last Moon was ready to make his upriver journey. Driving the dog salmon ahead of him, he cried, "The new generation is coming now and you shall be food for the people, O Dog Salmon!" At various stops along the way, he turned people who were fighting into stones, and turned others into sandpipers, sawbill ducks, mallards, and clams.

He found Deer making spearpoints of bone, singing, "This is what I am making to kill the Changer." But Moon turned the points into hooves, changing the would-be assassin into an ordinary deer. After giving all the animals their present form and establishing various features of the natural and social worlds, he reached his old home, joined his younger brother (who had been created from the diaper), and rose into the sky as the moon. His brother became the sun.

In concluding this version of the Moon cycle, told in the 1920s, the narrator commented, "I am an Indian today. Moon has given us fish and game. The white people have come and overwhelmed us. We may not kill a deer nor catch a fish forbidden by white men to be taken. I should like any of these lawmakers to tell me if Moon or Sun has set him here to forbid our people to kill game given to us by Moon and Sun. Though white people overwhelm us, it is Moon that placed us here, and the laws we are bound to obey are those established by Moon in the ancient time."

The narrator was referring to nineteenth-century treaties whereby Indians, yielding nearly all their lands, retained hunting and, especially, fishing rights. In the 1920s, in violation of the treaties, these rights were being transferred to commercial fishing companies operated by non-Indians. Not until the mid-1960s did the tide begin to turn, as the Coast Salish and neighboring tribes staged "fish-ins" along riverbanks in western Washington, eventually winning support from the United States Justice Department.

The question of fishing rights, still unresolved, has remained the single most important Indian issue in the Coast-Plateau region. As late as 1982 the Klamath tribe of southern Oregon found it necessary to file suit in federal court in order to reaffirm fishing, hunting, and trapping rights in their territory—winning a judgment in their favor in December of that year.

The root child

Among the Coeur d'Alene and other Interior Salish tribes, the Transformer was said to have been born to a young woman who married a hog-fennel root or, less euphemistically, used the root in an improper manner. The hero was sensitive about his peculiar origin and, according to some versions, transformed the creatures of the myth age for the simple reason that they insulted him.

In the topsy-turvy world of ancient times, Pestle Boy was a man-eater, as were Comb, Awl, and Bladder people—until Child of the Root changed them into the utensils of today. As the hero's adventures drew to a close, an amorous old toad woman tried to get close to him but was rebuffed. Luring him into her warm, comfortable house, she jumped on his face and stuck there. Unable to pull her off, he rose to the sky, becoming the moon, on whose face we may still see the toad.

In northwestern California, heroes were likewise supposed to have originated from edible roots. Here the story was that the young woman had been forbidden to dig a man-shaped root but did so anyway. When the thing cried like a baby, she took it home and raised it as her son. According to the Tolowa, this child became the culture hero, a monster slayer who roamed the countryside between the Rogue and the Klamath rivers. When his exploits were done, he rose to the sky.

South and east of the Tolowa, the story eventually becomes a mere folktale, called Dug-from-Ground, recounting the adventures of a nondescript hero who passes tests and wins a bride.

Musp and *Komól*

Until they were decimated by the cholera epidemic of 1830, the richest people in the region had been the Chinookan tribes of the lower Columbia River. With their surpluses of dried salmon they traded far up the river and along the coasts, bringing home goat-hair robes, elk hides, canoes, slaves, and exotic foods.

Along with the tangible imports came myths, including the important cycle of the twin transformers *Musp* and *Komól*, believed to have originated with the southern Coast Salish. Like most Transformer cycles of the Coast-Plateau, the epic began with a colorful folktale accounting for the heroes' origin, in this case a subtype of the Northwest Coast Bear Mother story, which will here be called The Bear Daughter.

A young woman, it seems, had been abducted by a grizzly bear. He carried her off to his den, and there she bore him a son and a daughter. Rescued by her five brothers, all but one of whom are killed in the violent confrontation with the bear and the bear's son, the woman sets out for home with her surviving brother and her bear daughter. Along the way she jumps into a lake and swims off as a seal.

Reaching the village accompanied by her mother's brother, the bear daughter is soon married to the village chief. But she is a laughing monster (people fall dead when she laughs) and also a devouring monster, who compulsively swallows the entire village the moment she has killed them with her laugh. Realizing she has lost her husband along with everyone else, she coughs him back up and hangs him on the wall in a basket. He is now legless.

Nevertheless she conceives, giving birth to two sons, *Musp* and *Komól,* whom she brings rapidly to manhood by bathing them constantly. Warned of her horrible traits by their father, who speaks to them from the basket, the heroes seize their mother by the hair and shake her bones out of her skin. The skin turns into a dog, who then becomes their faithful companion as they proceed through the country as transformers.

Many of their endless adventures play to the topsy-turvy theme. Finding people who do nothing but dance, they show them how to net flounder. When they meet a man who shoots at the rain to protect his house, because he has no roof, they build him a proper house. Discovering a tribe that walks on its hands, they show them how to walk upright.

In less whimsical episodes the brothers teach people how to catch salmon, spear whales, dig clams, gather cockles, and clean their houses. After saving people from an ogress, they throw the parts of her body in various directions, thus creating the different tribes. Their duties completed, they change into boulders, which may yet be seen.

Jesus the traveler

In 1926 the anthropologist Thelma Adamson obtained a few short Transformer tales from an old Salish man in the Chehalis River country of western Washington. These were told at least partly in English with "Jesus the traveler" as hero.

"My god!" exclaimed Jesus as he came to a man splitting logs using his hand as a wedge and his head as a maul. "What's going on here?" After demonstrating the proper way to make a wedge and maul, the hero traveled on and came to a fisherman who used women as posts to hold open his salmon trap. "What's going on here?" said Jesus, and he taught the people how to prop the trap open with willow poles. To save himself and others, he transformed the cannibal deer man and the beaver "who was making a nice butcher knife with which to kill Jesus." At other times he dropped fish bones into the rivers, creating salmon, suckers, and trout.

Although these episodes evidently belong to the Transformer cycle, Adamson tried to find out for sure whether the storyteller was substituting Jesus for the Transformer, Moon, or for the trickster, *Hwan.* The old man declined to give her an answer, but his wife, who was from the Puyallup country a little farther to the north, said, *"Hwan* is Jesus."

Immediately to the south, the Salishan Cowlitz considered *Hwan* the same as Coyote. Be that as it may, in the few tales that have been recorded, Jesus maintains the dignity and idealism of the Transformer, unmixed with the rascality of *Hwan* or Coyote.

Twelve

Making the World
As It Is

"All things good or bad"

Myths about the creation of the earth and the origin of death are
not normally included in the Coast-Plateau Transformer cycle.
Either they appear as independent stories or they are assigned to
the Trickster-Transformer, who is usually Coyote.

Coyote's fascination lies in his ability to bridge the gap between
the scurrilous and the divine. People feel that he stands for humanity. He is the advocate of death and the steadfast champion
of sexuality, yet by accident or design he is also the bringer of
food and sometimes the creator of the world. Usurping the role

of the Transformer, he even slays an occasional monster. Known throughout the west, he is perhaps most at home in the Coast-Plateau region, though he is not its only trickster.

Bluejay, a mere clown in Coast Salish lore, becomes a culture hero for several of the Interior Salish tribes, who once honored him in an annual Bluejay Dance. Hop-dancing until overwhelmed by Bluejay power, shamans fled twittering and had to be captured and brought back to the medicine lodge by their fellow tribesmen. After they had regained their senses, they were able to perform cures and answer wishes.

Other important Coyote-like tricksters of the region include Black Bear of the Alsea and South Wind of the Tillamook. Still others, like *Hwan* of the Coast Salish and *Kumúkumts* of the Klamath and the Modoc have names that cannot be translated, yet their relationship to Coyote is unmistakable.

Lost-Across-the-Ocean, the culture hero of the Yurok, Hupa, Karok, and Wiyot of northwestern California, also belongs in this category. According to a Hupa myth, the hero sprang from the earth, released deer and salmon, instituted childbirth, created landscape features, and started the Jumping Dance to counteract disease. After killing four eyeless old cannibals and transforming cannibal soaproots into food, he created tribes by defecation. Then he stole a young girl's food and overate to the point of discomfort. Birds saved him by pecking open his belly, and to reward them he gave them their attributes. A born traveler, he eventually reached the ocean and disappeared across the water. Shortly thereafter, he returned to arrange immortality for the coming generation of people but failed when a seductive woman lured him back across the ocean.

As a group these unheroic heroes, like Coyote—as we have seen—are responsible for "all things good or bad."

Coyote releases salmon

The story of how Coyote outwitted two women who kept salmon from swimming upstream, then himself made waterfalls to thwart the salmon at every village where maidens refused his proposals, was formerly told in the Interior Salish and Sahaptian areas and, in modified form, as far south as the Wailaki of northwestern California.

"In the beginning," according to a Sanpoil version, "Coyote had great power. He said to himself, 'Why remain in seclusion when I have so much power?' " Then he began to travel down the Columbia River. Along the way he met Sparrow, who was wearing a beaded warbonnet. Coveting it, Coyote killed him, put on the bonnet, and continued his journey as close to the water as possible so he could admire his reflection while walking along.

Hearing grouse children chattering in their own language, he thought they mocked him, so he blinded them by putting pitch over their eyes. In retaliation the grouse mother boomed at him from behind bushes as he passed near the edge of a bluff. Frightened, he fell into the river, changing into a basket in order to fall more lightly.

Floating downstream, he came to where the two women had built a dam to hold back the salmon. Admiring the pretty basket, they took it home to use as a dish. But each day the salmon in the dish mysteriously vanished, eaten by Coyote. Realizing the dish was enchanted, they threw it into the fire. Just then a little boy emerged from the flames, and the women, feeling motherly, adopted him.

One evening when the women came home from berrying, the child was gone. Rushing to the dam, they saw that the little boy had become a man. It was Coyote. He had broken the dam, and the salmon were now swimming upstream.

After changing the two women into a snipe and a killdeer, Coyote followed the salmon, giving them as gifts to villagers as he traveled along. He went up various smaller rivers, distributing fish, but wherever there were maidens who rejected his amorous advances he created waterfalls that kept the salmon away.

Coyote as Orpheus

Known throughout the United States and southern Canada, the Orpheus tale was especially popular in south central California and even more so in the Coast-Plateau region. Here it was regularly treated as a myth about the origin of eternal death, and the hero, if such he can be called, was usually Coyote.

As recited by a Chinook storyteller shortly after the turn of the century, the myth opens with the death of Coyote's wife. Eagle's wife has also died, and the two husbands decide to search for the lost women at the western edge of the world. "Do not mourn," said Eagle. "That will not bring your wife back. Get your moccasins ready, and we will go somewhere."

Reaching the dead land, the two find themselves in an enormous meeting lodge, lit by the moon, which can be seen lying on the floor. The dead, however, appear only at "night," when an old woman swallows the moon. Coyote and Eagle observe that their wives are among them.

The next day, after the old woman had disgorged the moon and the dead had vanished, Coyote built a huge wooden box and put into it leaves from every kind of plant. With Eagle's help he killed the old woman, put on her dress, and, when the time came, swallowed the moon. As usual, the dead appeared. But Eagle had placed the box just beyond the exit to the lodge, and when Coyote disgorged the moon they all filed out and were caught.

After Eagle had closed the lid and Coyote had thrown the moon into the sky, where it remained, they started back. Hearing his wife's voice, Coyote begged to carry the box. At last, when they were almost home, Eagle gave in and handed the box to Coyote. In his impatience to see his wife, he opened it, and all the dead rose up like a cloud and disappeared to the west.

"You see what you have done," said Eagle. "If we had brought them all the way back, people would not die forever, but only for a season, like these plants, whose leaves we have brought. Hereafter trees and grasses will die only in the winter, but in the spring they will be green again. So it would have been with the people."

Coyote and the bird nester

The widespread Bird Nester is another tale that reaches its fullest development in the Coast-Plateau region, and once again Coyote is a principal character. The tendency to link sexuality with acts of mythic creation comes to the fore in several variants of this myth, which is basically the story of Coyote's adultery with his son's two wives.

While Coyote is seducing the wives, the son, stranded at the top of a tree or a cliff, where he has been sent to fetch eagle nestlings, finds that he has access to the sky world. From there, according to the Interior Salish, he threw a few of his pubic hairs, which became Indian hemp, an important native source of fiber. In an uninhibited Coos version he created the proper temperature in a too hot sun by copulating with her, using an iced penis.

The more staid Klamath and Modoc variants have him promptly rescued from the tree by butterfly women, before he has a chance to indulge in creative acts. In these stories the adulterous father is *Kumúkumts,* and the son is called *Aísis*

In the Yurok area of northwest California, famous for one of the most materialistic societies in North America, the stranded hero descended without ceremony. But then, in a fit of pique over what had happened during his absence, he went from house to house, stealing everybody's money (dentalium shells, the standard currency). In an act of service to humanity, the adulterous father stole it back and redistributed it throughout the country. The myth therefore accounts for the money supply.

Making the earth

Except in the California-Oregon border area, creation myths on a grand scale were lacking among the Coast-Plateau tribes. Before the era of European influence, the Sahaptian and the Interior Salish may have had no such myths at all.

In western Washington there were a few tales of world creation, but they were anecdotal and not considered of great importance. One of these, The Woman Who Washed Her Face, tells of a dirty "woman" (really a thrush) who finally washed herself after repeated scoldings. As she did, the drops of water falling from her face caused a world flood. Then Muskrat dived for a piece of earth, which swelled until it was large enough to be a refuge for all the people. For his good offices, Muskrat was paid with a fur coat.

Along the same lines the Chinook had a myth about a woman who meant to marry Panther but married Beaver by mistake. Discovering her error, she left Beaver, who cried so hard that his tears flooded the earth. Again, Muskrat was the earth diver. But in this story, instead of bringing up a piece of mud, he lifted the entire world.

Another earth lifter was Gopher, who in a Klamath story raised mountains by burrowing underwater. When he opened his mouth to yawn, fish, roots, and berries came forth.

Such playful myths are far removed from the preachy origin tales that have been garnered from the Salish and Sahaptian of eastern Washington, Idaho, Montana, and adjacent Canada. This was the area of the so-called Dreamer religions, a succession of crisis cults that developed in the 1800s under pressure from Christianity. The actual sources for the myths are hard to pinpoint, however, and they no doubt stem at least partly from native lore.

In these stories there is a central figure often called Chief, Old One, or Sweathouse, who, in the poorest examples, is simply said to have made the world and everything in it. An unusually elaborate Okanagon version begins by telling how Old One made the earth out of a woman ("the soil is her flesh; the trees and vegetation are her hair; the rocks, her bones; and the wind is her breath"). Then Old One created people out of clay, who in time were expelled from the Garden of Eden. Eventually Old One sent his son, Jesus, to save the people, and it was Jesus who taught them to pray.

World origin myths have deeper roots among the tribes of the lower Oregon Coast, where the California high creator concept extends northward at least as far as the Coos. In a Chastacosta version the creator is *Howalâchi* (giver), who with his unnamed companion stood and waited on the primeval waters. As the darkness faded, an island white as snow came floating out of the east. On it were two trees, a redwood and an ash. Blowing tobacco smoke, the creator caused the trees to bud. Then something like drops of water fell on the ground, and grass began to come up. The creator made five cakes of mud and dropped them into the ocean one at a time. With each cake the bottom came closer to the surface until the whole world appeared.

A Tolowa variant explains that the creator "thought" the world into existence. In this case it came floating in from the south with the first redwood tree in its center.

A simpler Coos version has the creator and his companion procede directly to the business at hand by dropping the five cakes into the ocean. Again the land rises closer and closer to the surface until with the fifth cake the whole world is lifted.

Stories of this sort echo the theme of the five world ages, which serves as an organizing principle for the Coos Coyote cycle and for the creation cycle of the neighboring Kalapuya. The idea is that the world as we know it today was gradually perfected over the course of four earlier ages. The same theme has been reported from the Yuki, the Pomo, and the Wintu of north central California and from as far east as the Flathead of Montana.

Obviously there is a parallel with the ancient Aztec myth of five world ages and with the Southwest Emergence cycle that describes a progression through four underworlds. But the thread of similarity between these mythologies seems slender indeed when compared with their great differences.

Myths as formulas

A noteworthy exception to the usual northern California pattern occurs among the Yurok, the Hupa, and the Karok. These were the tribes that developed a sophisticated money economy and, in general, a material culture—with its stools, pillows, and purses—that could stand comparison with the civilizations of the Northwest Coast. Yet in this small area of high culture there was no high creator and very little speculation about ultimate origins.

Short on philosophy, the myths of the Yurok and their neigh-bors were rich in practical applications. Myths were recited for the purpose of curing sickness, warding off sterility, finding deer, and accumulating wealth. Nowhere else in North America were mythic narratives actually used as spells or formulas. In other words, an ordinary-sounding tale about the immortals of the ancient time would be told in place of a prayer.

To win a husband, for example, a Karok woman could tell the following *ikaréya* story (story about immortals). Once there were two young women living alone—so the story goes—and every day the younger woman went out for firewood while her sister stayed home pounding acorns. Yet no supply of acorns could be seen building up. Where could they be? Finally the one who had been going out said she would stay and make baskets while her sister packed wood. As soon as she was by herself, she looked behind the woodpile and found two dwarves. It was they who had been eating the acorns. Having suffered long enough from hunger, she picked up a stick and killed the two intruders.

But these dwarves were the wind children, and in revenge Wind blew the roof off the house and carried the young woman across the ocean. In her despair she wept aloud. Soon the culture hero, Lost-Across-the-Ocean, appeared, saying, "I heard you singing."

"I thought I was crying," she said. Then the culture hero off-ered to marry her and took her home—and with that she was well satisfied.

Such a story was called a "medicine." Any woman desiring a husband could recite it and thereby improve her chances for marriage. Unusual as it is, the formula or "medicine" story was not unique to northwestern California. Five thousand miles away the Arekuna Indians of eastern Venezuela developed the same kind of formula, called *tarén* in their language. Many of the Arekuna formulas were, and still are, used to ward off disease. A few are love charms.

Striking similarities separated by impressively great distances are one of the plagues of mythology. The temptation to link them historically or psychically is as easy to ridicule as it is hard to resist. Usually, however, we are talking about recurrent themes or motifs that jump out of the texts, like the five world ages of Aztec lore. In the case of narrative formulas the texts are silent. It is not what is said but the attitude toward it that sets up the mysterious parallel.

Part Six ↘

PLAINS

Thirteen

Father Creators
and Boy Heroes

Plains mythology at a glance

At the end of a session in which hero tales had been told, a
Wichita narrator of the old days, thinking back over his own life,
would weep, while his young listeners, thinking ahead, would
strike their front teeth with their thumbnails, indicating their
desire to live long and perform deeds like those that had just been
recounted. Then the storyteller would make an offering of food
and tobacco smoke to the mythical heroes and raise a pouch of
food to the Creator in the sky. The session would close with
offerings to the four directions and to the earth.

Such a ritual, with its strong human values and its attention to placement within a cosmic frame, is fully typical of the Plains. Elegantly ceremonious, this kind of lore may well have originated in the agricultural societies of the southeastern part of the region.

All Plains tribes, however, were hunters for at least a few months of the year, and the western and northern bands knew no other way of life, covering great distances on horseback as they followed the roaming buffalo herds.

Among groups devoted mainly or exclusively to hunting, the sky father addressed in prayers was usually different from the Creator described in myths. Nevertheless, even if known to be Coyote, the mythic creator could be spoken of as Father or Old Man. The Blackfeet called him—and still call him—*Napi* (old man); to the Crow he is Old Man Coyote. Several tribes know him as Spider.

The creation myth itself was usually The Earth Diver, with the Old Man supervising, as Muskrat or some other creature brought up the mud that formed the world. In other tales the Creator made humans, established death, obtained summer, struck fire, and taught the various arts. In one of the most popular stories he released the buffalo, which Crow had impounded in a cave. For the Comanche, who did not have The Earth Diver, this tale was the principal myth.

Still further stories show the Creator as a trickster who steals food, cheats on his wife, and plays the fool. Typical Plains trickster tales include The Women's Camp, The Mourner's Haircut, The Mice's Sun Dance, and Fat, Grease, and Berries. These are mostly trivial stories, told for entertainment.

Moving east and south into the territory of the Sioux, the Pawnee, and the Wichita, we find the trickster demoted to a subordinate role and the acts of creation taken over by loftier powers. The transition is signaled in certain Cheyenne and Gros Ventre stories in which the earth diver becomes the animal helper of a remote "being" or "person," not the usual trickster-creator. East and south the Earth Diver tale itself drops out, emergence themes appear, and the creation of the world is said to have been the work of a spirit called *Tiráwahat* by the Pawnee, Man Never

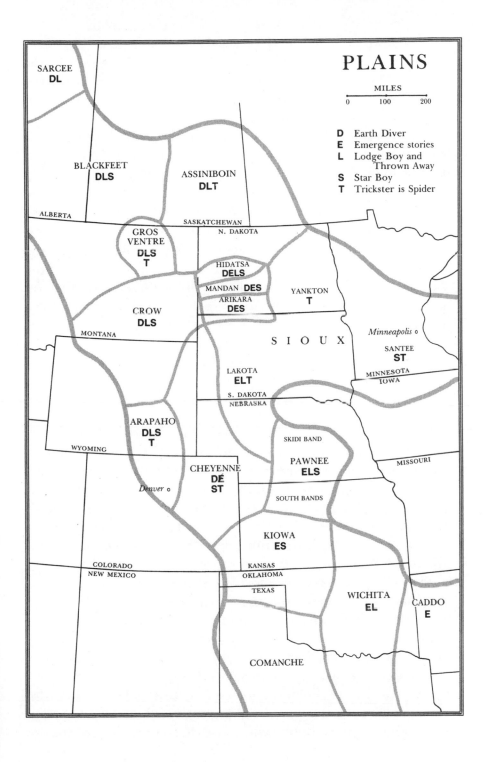

PLAINS

MILES

0   100   200

D Earth Diver
E Emergence stories
L Lodge Boy and
    Thrown Away
S Star Boy
T Trickster is Spider

SARCEE
DL

BLACKFEET
DLS

ASSINIBOIN
DLT

ALBERTA

SASKATCHEWAN

N. DAKOTA

GROS
VENTRE
**DLS
T**

HIDATSA
DELS

MANDAN **DES**

ARIKARA
DES

YANKTON
T

CROW
DLS

MONTANA

Minneapolis o

S I O U X

SANTEE
ST

LAKOTA
ELT

MINNESOTA
IOWA

S. DAKOTA
NEBRASKA

ARAPAHO
**DLS
T**

WYOMING

SKIDI BAND

PAWNEE
ELS

MISSOURI

CHEYENNE
**DÉ
ST**

Denver o

SOUTH BANDS

KIOWA
ES

COLORADO
NEW MEXICO

KANSAS
OKLAHOMA

TEXAS

WICHITA
EL

CADDO
E

COMANCHE

Known on Earth by the Wichita, and Great Father Above by the Caddo. These personages are never tricksters. After setting the stage, the remote originator usually withdraws, having transferred his powers to a first man, who becomes the culture bringer.

But creation cycles did not represent the whole mythology of this region. Just as important, if not more so, were the hero tales that brought tears to the narrator's eyes and stirred the young men to high deeds on the warpath and in the hunt. Among the Pawnee such stories were called *kawaharu* (fortune) tales, because they were thought to bring luck. In several of the western and northern tribes the telling of them developed into a refined art, with results that could be compared to the novelistic tales of the Zuni and the Iroquois. Though they have variants in other regions, these are the myths that are most characteristic of the Plains.

The unpromising hero

"There was a poor, lame, one-eyed boy, whose hair was bushy, because he never had anybody to brush it. He had many lice. People hated him, because he was dirty." So begins a Pawnee tale, with a string of pejoratives perhaps lengthier than was customary. Yet it omits the information—commonly given in such stories— that the hero suffered from skin sores, that he had no relatives, and that the other boys urinated on his miserable little lodge whenever they passed by.

Plains heroes were not born to succeed. Even their names proclaimed their humble origins: Scarface, Found-in-the-Grass, Dirty Boy, Thrown Away. More than a few Cheyenne tales were told of Pot Belly. Among the Wichita, favorites were Little-Big-Belly-Boy, Wets-the-Bed, and Half-a-Boy (who "had a hard time in his early life, and that kept him from growing").

The Cinderella theme is not limited to the Plains. Rags-to-riches stories are also popular along the Northwest Coast and in most other regions. But nowhere else do so many heroes start so low.

Lodge Boy and Thrown Away

One of the best known of the boy-hero myths, told throughout the Plains from Canada to Texas, begins with a husband's warning to his pregnant wife. She must be careful not to receive guests while he is away. Yet, when a strange man appears, she breaks the prohibition and invites him into the lodge. In some versions the visitor is Double Face, a monster with eyes, nose, and mouth on the back of his head.

The woman serves him meat in a bark dish, but Double Face says, "No, I do not take my food from bark." She tries a bowl of buffalo horn, then sheep horn, then moose, without success. Finally he allows her to understand that the food must be laid on her abdomen, and she complies. As he carves the meat, he cuts into her body, killing her, at the same time delivering her twin sons. Before departing, he throws one of the boys into the spring, leaving the other inside the lodge.

When the husband returns, he buries his wife; and finding a child in the lodge, he feeds him, and the boy grows rapidly. The other child, Thrown Away, comes inside to eat and to play with his brother, but only when the father is absent. At last the man catches his second son and, according to a Crow version, takes the wildness out of him by burning incense under his nose. With that "he became human."

Ready for adventure, the boys learn of various monsters from their father, who describes each danger, then orders them to avoid it. As soon as the father is out of sight, the twins head for the thunderbird nest or the swallowing monster or whatever peril has just been forbidden. In every case they triumph, even putting an end to Double Face, who had killed their mother.

In some versions they exhume the mother's body and bring her back to life. (The entire sequence concerning Double Face and the twins is reminiscent of a northwestern California myth in which children of the ancient time were born by cesarean section, always killing the mother, until the culture hero established natural childbirth.)

According to a Wichita storyteller, the twins killed all the evil creatures that lived in the ancient time. Returning from their last, long adventure, they found their father gone (he had become a star) and their lodge grown over with vines. Thrown Away shot an arrow into the distance, and a drop of blood fell on his hand, showing that the star was the boys' father. Having understood this signal, they climbed through the air and joined their father in the night sky.

But as told by the Sarcee, Blackfeet, Gros Ventre, and Arapaho, the twins' final exploit merely forms a bridge to a second saga, called Dirty Boy or Found-in-the-Grass. In a Blackfeet version, Thrown Away climbed a stretching tree to the upper world and disappeared. In his loneliness the deserted brother cried so hard that he was transformed, becoming "a dirty little ragged boy."

An old woman took pity on him and led him to her tent. But she harbored no illusions about his chances in life. When the chief of the camp announced a shooting contest to determine who would win his beautiful daughter, and Dirty Boy asked the old woman to make him arrows so that he could compete, she said, "Oh, you dirty thing! You are a disgrace to the camp, you would nauseate everybody." Nevertheless she made him a bow and four arrows, though very poor ones. With these, need it be said, he won the contest.

After further adventures, Dirty Boy transformed himself into a handsome man, saved his starving tribe by rounding up buffalo, then rose to the sky and joined his brother, the two becoming the stars Castor and Pollux.

The classic Blackfeet version, here summarized all too briefly, was told to the anthropologist Clark Wissler and members of his party in the year 1903 by the narrator Wolf Head (born 1840), two years before his death. "Wolf Head understood that these myths would be published eventually," wrote Wissler, "and as he proceeded we realized that he was making the artistic effort of his life."

Star Boy

It is doubtful that Lodge Boy and Thrown Away was ever the principal myth of any Plains tribe, despite its popularity. However, the comparable tale of Star Boy did achieve that rank, or near it, for several tribes, including the Crow, Arapaho, Blackfeet, and Kiowa.

The epic starts with the Star Husband tale (which also introduces the Coast-Plateau myth of *Musp* and *Komól*). Thus there are two girls, wishing for star husbands, who wake up in the sky world, one of them pregnant. After descending to earth with her newborn son, the young mother dies, and the child becomes a hero.

Or the introduction is a subtype of The Star Husband, in which one of the girls is lured to the sky by a beautiful porcupine who climbs a stretching tree. Usually the porcupine is the moon in disguise, sometimes the sun. The young woman marries him, bears a son, and descends or falls back to earth. In these versions the hero child is often called Moon Boy or Sun Boy. In a Crow variant the sky husband is said to be the Creator. But this interesting connection is seldom made.

After his mother's death, the boy is adopted by an old woman, who becomes the most important female character in the story. Variously called Grandmother, Old Woman Night, or Old Woman Who Never Dies, she is an earth mother or a vegetation goddess, reminiscent of the Navajo Changing Woman. As in Southwest hero myths, she sends the boy out on his adventures, and he continually returns to her lodge.

Star Boy's exploits are similar to those of Lodge Boy and Thrown Away. In fact, several of the episodes are interchangeable. In addition to the thunderbird and the swallowing monster, the heroes of both myths come to grips with Long Arms, Fire Moccasins, and the female Pot Tilter (who kills people by tipping a cauldron of boiling water).

Unlike Lodge Boy and Thrown Away, who sometimes revive their mother, Star Boy himself undergoes death and resurrection. A snake enters his body and remains there until the boy is dead. His flesh falls away, but still the snake stays coiled among the bones. As long as it is there, the hero cannot return to life. In a Gros Ventre version the Moon father finally takes pity on his son and sends a cold rain, which drives the snake out. Immediately the boy stands up, fully restored.

During the time that he lay as an (outstretched?) skeleton, "he gave his image to the people as a cross"—according to an Arapaho storyteller, perhaps under Christian influence. Then he rose into the sky, becoming "the morning star, so called the cross, but really the Little Star [i.e., Star Boy]."

Among the Blackfeet the protagonist of the tale is the tribal hero, called Scarface. His adventures are son-in-law tests, and, as in the case of Dirty Boy, his reward is a beautiful bride. According to the Kiowa, the hero early in his career divides into two, called Split Boys. In the end, one of the Split Boys disappears under a lake, while the other transforms himself into the *tsaidetali* medicines, which are the sacred bundles, or portable altars, of the Kiowa.

The Sun Dance

"My grandfather, Light of the World; Old Woman Night, my grandmother, I stand here before this people, old and young." With these words the medicine man opened a typical prayer of the Arapaho Sun Dance, invoking the old woman who had adopted Star Boy.

For most Plains tribes the Sun Dance, held in late spring or early summer, was the principal ceremony of the year. Partly a social occasion, it was also an opportunity for people to renew their faith in the spirits and for men to demonstrate their powers of endurance. Accordingly, its four days of complex ritual contained allusions to the boy-hero myths. Among the Blackfeet the Sun Dance itself was said to have been instituted by Scarface, whereas the Hidatsa gave credit to Thrown Away, whose final adventure in their version of the story was a journey to the sky world, where the hero learned the various rites.

The Arapaho also paid tribute to the tale of Lodge Boy and Thrown Away, but in subtler fashion, placing a special knife on the Sun Dance altar, said to have been the knife used by the monster in performing the cesarean section on the heroes' mother. In addition the Arapaho honored the mother of Star Boy, identifying the center pole in the Sun Dance lodge with the tree the young heroine climbed as she followed the porcupine.

The most spectacular feature of the Sun Dance, at least as practiced by the Arapaho, the Sioux, and several other tribes, was the self-sacrifice of one or more participants, who allowed skewers to be inserted through the flesh of the shoulders and the chest. The skewers were tied to buffalo skulls, which pulled at the wounds as the men danced. Or the dancers were attached to long cords running from the skewers to the center pole or to the rafters of the lodge. Either the men strained against the cords while dancing, or they were raised several feet above the ground and remained suspended. In the Arapaho rites the cords represented the rope used by Star Boy's mother in her descent from sky to earth.

Shocked nineteenth-century observers condemned the practice, calling it unchristian, and the Sun Dance was outlawed in 1881. Although it was reinstated by the Indian Reorganization Act of 1934, the rite of sacrifice was still generally excluded until the 1960s, when it at last returned in full force. With changing attitudes, the old Sun Dance "torture," today referred to as the "immolation" or the "penitential feature," can be shown in television documentaries and spoken of dispassionately even by Christian missionaries.

Okipa

At the same time that it commemorates the boy heroes, the Sun Dance recalls the acts of the father creator. Among the Arapaho and the Cheyenne, clumps of sod are placed on the principal altar as a means of reenacting the Earth Diver myth. In a sense the entire Sun Dance is a world renewal ceremony in which both nature and society are given a new lease on life.

Next two pages. Two body paintings from the Mandan *Okipa,* as sketched by George Catlin in 1832: (1) buffalo bull and (2) Foolish Doer.

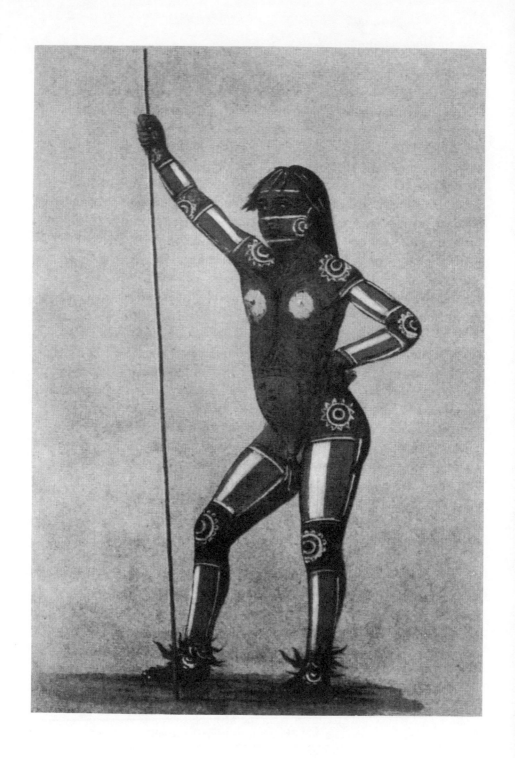

Perhaps no version of the Sun Dance has made this point so dramatically as the four-day *Okipa* of the Mandan, formerly held each year as soon as the willow leaves were fully expanded. Loosely based on the myth of the creator-provider Lone Man, the ritual consisted of masques and dances that tied in with the narrative episodes.

Briefly, the epic of Lone Man is the story of world creation, as usual by means of the earth diver, followed by Lone Man's release of the buffalo that had been impounded by Speckled Eagle. Next comes the world flood, from which Lone Man rescues the people by building a watertight stockade around the village. Finally there is the birth of the monster slayer, Foolish Doer, whose power to kill evil creatures frightens the other spirits, who unite to destroy him. After sealing Foolish Doer in a tomb of black rock, Lone Man departs, saying, "When people think of me, I will answer as the south wind."

Anyone familiar with Indian lore has seen reproductions of the paintings by George Catlin of the *Okipa* he witnessed in 1833. These show the domed earth lodges of the Mandan clustered around an open plaza, in the center of which is the tall barrel-like structure of planks representing the stockade that saved the people from the flood. The figures of the buffalo dancers and the ceremonial clown, Foolish Doer, black all over with a superimposed pattern of white circles, show that the art of Mandan body painting had reached a high degree of perfection.

The accompanying myths were not fully reported until a hundred years later, at which time they were still intact, though the ceremony had lapsed. Catlin himself, who preserved a few mythic fragments, could well have done better. "I might write much more on them," he noted, "giving yet a volume on their stories and traditions; but it would be a volume of fables, and scarce worth recording."

Fourteen

Earth and Sky

The heavy woman

The Hidatsa of western North Dakota were the northernmost of the Plains tribes to grow corn and live in permanent villages. According to their mythology, adapted from the Mandan, they emerged from the earth carrying their garden produce with them. Lone Man was their leader.

A vine they had planted in the underworld had grown through a hole in the earth's crust, and it was this that they climbed as they made their way upward, one by one. Many had already emerged when a pregnant woman began the ascent. Others still waited below, but this woman was so heavy she broke the vine, with the result that she and the rest remained in the underworld.

In one of the Mandan accounts, virgins are mentioned as having made the ascent, and the heavy woman is said to have been forbidden to try. Hers was an act of defiance that resulted in the permanent separation of the people, the lower group representing the dead; the upper, the living.

The same story has been recorded among the Lakota Sioux and, in much weaker form, among the Cheyenne. An old Kiowa version has it that the people emerged one by one through a hollow log, somewhere far to the north. But when a pregnant woman tried to squeeze through, she became stuck, blocking the way for those behind her.

With the insight of a poet, the modern Kiowa writer N. Scott Momaday has retold this myth in his memoir *The Way to Rainy Mountain,* relating it to the sudden awareness he imagines having come over him at some point in his personal past. "Yes, I thought, now I see the earth as it really is; never again will I see things as I saw them yesterday or the day before."

The woman between

With the Arikara, whose villages lay immediately to the south of the Mandan, the emergence story took a somewhat different form. According to the sacred words of the myth, the first beings made by *Nishánu* (chief) were giants, who had to be destroyed because they mocked their creator. After putting a few of his favorites in the ground as corn kernels, *Nishánu* drowned the others in a world flood. He also planted corn in the sky, and when it matured he took an ear and turned it into Mother Corn, who came down from the sky world to lead the new people up out of the ground.

In those days the people were still animals, and some, like the badger and the mole, were able to help Mother Corn by tunneling upward through the earth. This occurred far to the east. When the people had emerged, the mother led them westward past three obstacles (a chasm, a thick forest, a lake), then left them to their own devices as she returned to the sky.

In her absence the people played shinny and the hoop and pole game, and both games ended in fighting and killing. *Nishánu* was displeased. He sent Mother Corn back to earth with a man to be the people's leader, "whose name should be *Nishánu.*" This man showed them how to make war on their enemies, and Mother Corn herself taught them their tribal rituals.

The idea of a female figure who mediates between heaven and earth recurs among the closely related Pawnee, who worshipped the evening star in this role, and among the Lakota Sioux, whose White Buffalo Calf Woman is probably a late adaptation of either an Arikara or a Pawnee model. In the words of an old-time Arikara narrator, "Reverence and gratitude are due from mankind to *Nishánu Natchitak* (chief above) for all good things which we have, and to Mother Corn, through whose mediation we enjoy all these benefits."

Tiráwahat

The recitation of the Arikara genesis myth occurred during the spring creation rite, at which time the sacred bundle of Mother Corn, containing ears of corn and other objects wrapped in a buffalo skin, was carefully opened. As the Arikara used to say, "Mother has undone her belt."

In their own creation ceremony, held at approximately the same time, the Skidi Pawnee unwrapped their Evening Star, or Yellow Buffalo Calf, bundle, also containing ears of corn, as well as a sacred pipe. In a ritual that included prayers to Mother Corn, variously called Mother of the Dawn and Mother Sunset Yellow, the Skidi priests chanted a poetic version of the genesis myth, symbolically re-creating the world, step by step. A narrated version recorded in 1902, after the ceremony had become nearly extinct, tells the following story.

In the beginning there was *Tiráwahat* (expanse), who spoke to the gods that sat around him, directing them to their proper places. Sun was sent to the east, Moon to the west. To the Evening Star he said, "You shall stand in the west; you shall be known as Mother of all things, for through you all beings shall be created." The Morning Star he placed in the east to be the warrior that drives the "people" (the stars?) toward the west. The North Star and another, unidentified star were stationed in the north and the south respectively.

Then *Tiráwahat* assigned four others to be the stars of the northeast, northwest, southwest, and southeast, telling them to hold up the sky. "Your powers will be known by the people, for you shall touch the heavens with your hands, and your feet shall touch the earth."

When all the gods had been instructed in their duties, *Tiráwahat* gave Clouds, Winds, Lightnings, and Thunders to the Evening Star and told her to place them between herself and her garden (a mythical cornfield in the west). As these four shook their gourd rattles and sang, *Tiráwahat* began creating the earth.

"Clouds came up. The winds blew the clouds. The lightnings and thunders entered the clouds. The clouds were placed over the space, and as the clouds were now thick, [*Tiráwahat*] dropped a pebble into them. The pebble was rolled around in the clouds. When the storm had passed over, there was in the space all water." Then the four sky-supporters struck the water with their war clubs, separating it so that earth appeared.

After the streams were cleaned and the various seeds quickened, the Evening Star took the Morning Star as her consort, and the pair produced a girl to be the mother of humanity. Moon and Sun produced a boy to be the girl's husband. Then Evening Star showed the husband how to make the sacred bundle, and the four elements under Evening Star's control (Clouds, Winds, Lightnings, and Thunders) taught the songs of all the ceremonies.

In the condensed imagery of the creation-rite songs, the role of the four elements is taken over by *Paruhti* (wonderful being), another name for *Tiráwahat,* imagined as traveling over the dead earth bringing everything to life. The spring thunder was said by the Skidi Pawnee to have been the voice of *Paruhti,* and the rite itself was called the Thunder Ceremony.

The Greek connection

With its orderly pantheon and its firm ties to ritual and theology, the Skidi creation tale comes very close to the old-fashioned European idea of what myth ought to be. The story was recorded only once, however, from the priest Roaming Scout, as interpreted by the half-Pawnee ethnographer James R. Murie, himself an Episcopalian.

Murie has been accused of inaccurate translation and, more insidiously, of presenting his materials in what has been called a favorable light. But since these charges are neither conclusive nor unusual, and in view of Murie's massive contributions to Pawnee and Arikara studies, there can be no harm in believing that the classical overtones in the mythology of *Tiráwahat* are the work of coincidence rather than design.

No doubt a taste for the classical had currency during those years. In his *Dakota Grammar* of 1893, Stephen Return Riggs enthusiastically likened the water monster of Santee Sioux myth to the Greek god Poseidon and the thunderbird to Jupiter Tonans. Alongside his folkloristic texts, though, the comparisons seem strained.

A few years later the physician-ethnographer J. R. Walker had better luck among the Lakota Sioux. Working with sophisticated medicine men, the last of whom died in the 1920s, Walker pieced together a systematic mythology that "is much like that of ancient Egypt, Greece, and Rome." And this time it really is. But the method is questionable. Having immersed himself in Lakota lore, Walker apparently built myths out of scraps of conversations and answers to leading questions that he had posed.

The most that can be claimed is that he created nothing out of whole cloth. Thus whatever he has to say is, in a sense, authentic.

In Walker's cosmogony the mystical figure *Skan* (untranslatable, identified with the sky) corresponds to the Skidi *Tiráwahat*, and the female mediator is now *Wohpe* (meteor), also called White Buffalo Calf Woman. *Skan*, the Great Spirit, created *Wohpe* as his daughter and made her the goddess of harmony, beauty, and pleasure.

At first, however, there was only *Inyan* (rock), who used his own body to create the great disk *Maka* (earth). As the blood flowed from his veins, forming the waters of the earth, *Inyan* shrank, becoming hard and powerless. A portion of the waters became *Tanka* (sky). Then a voice said, "I am the source of energy, I am *Skan.*"

After creating *Anp* (light) and *Wi* (sun), *Skan* called a council of the gods and gave them the power to originate more gods and goddesses, evidently to assuage a general feeling of loneliness. In short order the story becomes caught up in a series of amorous intrigues among the gods and first mortals, with all the scheming and partner-switching of Greek mythology.

In the 1930s Franz Boas sent his student Ella Deloria, herself a Sioux, to find out if Walker's stories could be verified. They could not. No one in South Dakota remembered a mythology of this sort. Possibly it had been the secret property of a few shamans. And perhaps it was not traditional. As has been pointed out more than once, Walker's principal source, though he was a medicine man, was the Episcopal deacon George Sword.

Nevertheless, at least one of these curious tales was remembered in the 1970s by the medicine man Lame Deer, who had heard it from his grandmother. As recorded by Walker, it is a story of *Wi,* who cheated on his wife, *Hanwi* (moon). *Wi* was attracted to the mortal woman *Ite* (face), who in turn betrayed her husband, *Tate* (wind). As punishment for their infidelity, *Skan* decreed that *Wi* would lose the companionship of *Hanwi*—thus Sun and Moon rule separate times of the day—and *Ite* would acquire a second, hideous face and be called *Anog-Ite* (double face, presumably no relation to the Double Face who murdered the mother of Lodge Boy and Thrown Away).

The villain of the piece, incidentally, is the trickster *Inktomi,* who arranged the illicit affair between *Wi* and *Ite.* But the story is hardly a trickster tale. Nor is the flavor entirely Greek. A trace of Victorian morality seems to be present. Moreover, like many of the tales in Walker's collections, it has the breathless quality of a plot summary rather than the easy flow of narrative. For reasons that are not hard to find, modern Lakota have approached Walker's mythology with a certain amount of caution. Most would agree, however, that it contains valuable insights into Lakota religious thought of the late nineteenth century—a period of great creativity for the Sioux, just as it was for the tribes of north central California.

Fifteen

Myths for the Future

Doomsday

During the Ghost Dance activity of 1890, prophecies of world destruction swept through the Plains. People thought the earth was about to be destroyed and a new earth would come gliding out of the sky, bringing back the buffalo. The whites would vanish, and all the Indian ancestors—the ghosts—would return to life.

Earlier, in the Coast-Plateau region, similar visions had inspired the mystical Dreamer cults, which spilled into Nevada and extended as far north as the Athapascan Carrier and Beaver Indians. Some had said that lakes and rivers would undermine the earth and set it free like an island, just as in the ancient time. Then Coyote would return to destroy the whites and make the world the happy place it once had been.

Doomsday myths go hand in hand with religions like the Ghost Dance that spring up in times of crisis, and often they fade from memory after the excitement has passed. It would appear, however, that these prophecies are sometimes a permanent part of a tribe's mythology. Among the Lakota and the Pawnee, for example, there is a story that after the primeval flood the Creator placed a buffalo in the north to hold back the waters. Every year this buffalo loses one hair. When its hairs are all gone, the world will be flooded again.

According to the Wichita, life on earth as we know it today began in the ancient time when a voice called out to Star That Is Always Moving, telling him to shoot the last of three deer that were to leap out of the water. The first deer was white; the second, black; and the last, black-and-white. The shooting of the black-and-white deer signified the alternation of night and day, which had not yet been regulated. The hunter wounded the deer and followed it and the two others into the sky, where they remain as a constellation. The man whose voice had instructed him became the sun.

After that, villages grew up, and the people were taught to hunt and plant corn. But Star That Is Always Moving still chases the three deer, hoping to retrieve his arrow, and every year he gets closer. When at last he catches the black-and-white deer, the world will come to an end. Then all the stars and the sun will become human beings again, as in the earliest time, and a new world will be created.

Tribal medicine

Sacred objects that symbolize the luck, or "medicine," of a tribe are especially important in the central Plains. For the Arapaho this medicine is the Flat Pipe. For the Suhtai Cheyenne it is the

Buffalo Cap, and for the Cheyenne proper, the four Sacred Arrows. These are real, physical objects, lovingly wrapped in sacred bundles, each with its appointed keeper. So long as the object remains intact, it has the power to carry its people into the future.

In the late twentieth century, tribal medicines continue to be venerated as objects of political if not religious value, and the myths that account for their origins are among the most vital and the most likely to survive. To a certain extent these stories deserve to be called legends rather than myths, since they often have a historical quality about them, which suggests comparison with the saints' legends of Christianity.

Arapaho tales that account for the origin of the Flat Pipe, however, are mythic in the pure sense. According to one of these stories, the pipe was brought up from beneath the water by the turtle, who played the part of the earth diver at the beginning of the world. In another version, the Creator is walking over the primeval water, holding the pipe and saying, "I do wish that there would be a land where I could keep [this pipe] holy and reverently." In answer to his prayer, birds and animals come from the four directions and take turns diving for earth. In still another version the pipe itself is the Creator, who floats on the water, "fasting and weeping and crying." Eventually the water animals come and dive for earth.

At the time of the Ghost Dance many Arapaho held the Flat Pipe uppermost in their thoughts, singing, "The sacred pipe tells me we shall surely be put again [with our dead friends and ancestors, soon to return]."

More typical, perhaps, is the Suhtai legend of the Buffalo Cap, which tells how the hero Erect Horns brought this lifesaving talisman to his people during a famine. Ostensibly the story dates from before 1850, at which time the Suhtai became a part of the

_____

Opposite page and following two pages. Three scenes from the legend of the Buffalo Cap: (1) the hero selects a companion, (2) they receive instruction at the sacred mountain, and (3) they return leading the buffalo. Drawings by Richard Davis, Cheyenne, 1901–1905.

Cheyenne. At some point in their early history, so it is said, the grass withered, the game animals died, and the people had nothing to live on but dried vegetation and dog meat.

In search of food, the people traveled north, camping one evening beside a stream. There the men of the tribe were directed to go in pairs toward women they admired and beg for something to eat. A young medicine man chose the wife of the chief, then promptly took her as his partner on a journey farther north. At night they made camp, but did not lie together. After several days these two approached a mountain, which they entered by rolling back a rock that had concealed a doorway. Inside, the Great Medicine taught them the songs and procedures of the Sun Dance, then said, "Take this horned cap to wear when you perform the ceremony that I have given you, and you will control the buffalo and all the other animals. Put the cap on as you go from here and the earth will bless you."

The couple did as they had been told, and as they came away from the mountain, driving their dogs in front of them, the buffalo fell in behind and the dead earth turned green. When the people saw the hero coming, wearing the Buffalo Cap, they named him Erect Horns.

The legend of the Sacred Arrows, which belongs to the Cheyenne proper, is nearly identical in its basic outline. Again the hero —here his name is Sweet Medicine—journeys with a bride and enters a mountain, where he acquires ceremonial knowledge. Accompanied by the bride, he returns with the medicine arrows, which the people have guarded to this day.

Both legends are reminiscent of the old and widespread Plains myth known as The Buffalo Wife, in which a young man marries a buffalo woman, who leads him to her homeland. There the buffalo show the hero how to eat buffalo meat and use a bow. Having learned this lesson, he returns home to teach his people.

White Buffalo Calf Woman

Undoubtedly the best known of the tribal medicines is the Calf Pipe of the Lakota Sioux. The story of its origin, in which a beautiful woman appears to a young man who is forbidden to touch her, bears a certain similarity to the Cheyenne legends but probably comes directly from one of the Caddoan tribes— Arikara, Pawnee, Wichita, or Caddo.

In fact a parallel myth has been recorded among the Wichita, and the Calf Pipe itself, which has a winglike flange on either side of the bowl, is of an Arikara type. According to old Sioux winter counts, it would seem that the pipe reached the Lakota between 1785 and 1800, perhaps not long after the Lakota had reached their present homeland in western South Dakota. It is well to keep in mind that the Sioux, like the Cheyenne, were latecomers to the Plains region, where the Caddoans had been long established.

According to the version told in 1907 by the medicine man Elk Head, who was then keeper of the pipe, the Lakota had formerly lived beside a lake far to the east. After a terrible winter, they began migrating westward, sending two scouts in advance. One of these two young men was good-hearted, the other bad.

Within sight of a low hill the scouts shot a deer. Just then the outline of a woman appeared in the mist that rose above the hill. As the mist lifted, they saw a beautiful maiden dressed in sage, holding a buffalo-skin bundle.

Overcome by lust, the bad-hearted man rushed toward the maiden. She warned him away, but he persisted. Suddenly the mist descended, and there was a hissing of rattlesnakes. When it cleared again, the other young man, who had been watching, saw that his companion had been reduced to bones.

The holy woman then ordered a circle of green boughs to be constructed and said she would reappear when the entire tribe had gathered there. The young man ran back with the message, the circle was prepared, and the next morning the maiden entered it.

Before all the people she unwrapped the pipe and taught the songs and prayers of five great ceremonies: the Fosterparent Chant, the Sun Dance, the Vision Cry, the Buffalo Chant, and the Ghost Keeper. Finally she said, "When you as a people cease to reverence the pipe, then you will cease to be a nation." With these words she disappeared, and the people saw only a white buffalo cow trotting over the prairie.

As in Elk Head's time, the pipe bundle today is kept at the Cheyenne River Reservation in northern South Dakota, where it is the object of pilgrimages. For the Lakota, all medicine pipes are related to the Calf Pipe, and virtually everyone in the tribe knows the legend of the White Buffalo Calf Woman. In contrast to the sacred lore of some groups, which is held secret or shared only at proper moments, the Calf legend can be told without ceremony, and almost anyone who knows it will tell it gladly.

Part Seven ↳

EAST

Lost Worlds of
the Southeast

Children of the sun

In the early 1700s, when the French began to settle Louisiana, they came in contact with a spectacular remnant of the temple-mound culture that had once dominated the region south of the Ohio River from the Mississippi to the Atlantic. This was the Natchez tribe, with its ruling Sun clan, its monarch, and its temples reminiscent of Aztec and Maya pyramids. Within thirty years the French destroyed the Natchez towns; and the culture known to archaeologists as the Mississippian, already in a long decline, effectively came to an end.

The next hundred years saw the gradual rise of the Creek, Cherokee, Choctaw, Chickasaw, and Seminole, who, with their enviable mastery of the white plantation economy, came to be labeled the five civilized tribes. In the 1830s, no longer tolerating competition from Indians, many of whom had become wealthy landholders, southern whites enforced the notorious policy of Removal, causing an Indian exodus unparalleled in American history. Following a "trail of tears" through Alabama, Mississippi, and Arkansas, thousands died as they were forced to vacate their ancestral territory—on foot and without sufficient food for their journey. Once again the native people of the Southeast were obliged to make a fresh start.

In their new homes in Oklahoma and Texas and in remote corners of the Old South where a few groups had found refuge, Indian elders gave occasional interviews to historians and anthropologists and in this way preserved what had remained to them of their old traditions. The last of the great collectors were Jack Frederic Kilpatrick and Anna Gritts Kilpatrick, themselves Cherokee, who continued to find myths, folktales, and incantations through the 1950s and into the 1960s.

From these records and from reports written by travelers and missionaries before Removal, it is possible to glimpse the mythology that rationalized the old cultures, even going back to the temple-mound era.

For the Chitimacha, whose towns lay south of the Natchez, it was the creator Thoumé who taught the people to make clothing, drill fire, and reproduce. After the creation of the moon and the sun, Thoumé sent a subordinate spirit to teach the arts of medicine and food preparation. Presumably this second spirit is the same as the trickster deity *Kútnahin,* who traveled all over the earth in the guise of a filthy person covered with buzzard dung. Once he peeped into a house and so frightened a man that he fled. *Kútnahin* shouted, "Don't be afraid. It is I, *Kútnahin.* " But the man would not listen and kept on into the forest.

The Natchez themselves, like the Incas of Peru, believed the arts of civilization had been taught by a man and a woman, descended from the sun. For the Creek, who lived east of the Nat-

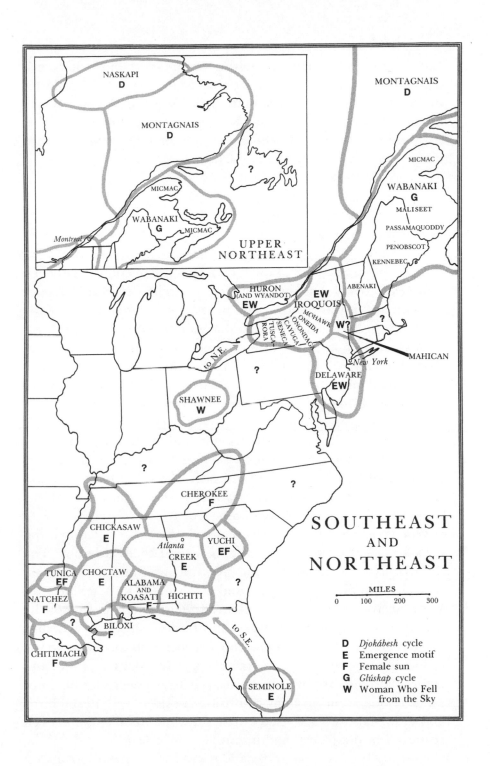

NASKAPI
D

MONTAGNAIS
D

MONTAGNAIS
D

MICMAC

WABANAKI
G

MICMAC

MICMAC

WABANAKI
G

MALISEET

PASSAMAQUODDY

PENOBSCOT

KENNEBEC

Montreal

UPPER
NORTHEAST

ABENAKI

HURON
(AND WYANDOT)
EW

EW

IROQUOIS

MOHAWK
ONEIDA
ONONDAGA
CAYUGA
SENECA
TUSCA-
RORA

W?

to N.E.

?

?

MAHICAN

New York

DELAWARE
EW

SHAWNEE
W

?

?

CHEROKEE
F

SOUTHEAST

AND

NORTHEAST

CHICKASAW
E

Atlanta
CREEK
E

YUCHI
EF

TUNICA
EF

CHOCTAW
E

ALABAMA
AND
KOASATI
F

HICHITI

?

MILES

0   100   200   300

NATCHEZ
F

?

BILOXI
F

to S.E.

CHITIMACHA
F

SEMINOLE
E

D *Djokábesh* cycle
E Emergence motif
F Female sun
G *Glúskap* cycle
W Woman Who Fell
       from the Sky

chez, culture had originated in the teachings of four deities, evidently the spirits of the four cardinal points, sent by the Master of Breath. Well into the twentieth century the Yuchi of Oklahoma, formerly of Georgia and South Carolina, remembered that their old way of life had been given to them by the sun, who had named them *tsoyahá* (children of the sun).

The lucky hunter and the corn mother

It might be supposed that the old Mississippian culture had been built exclusively on agriculture. But archaeological evidence shows that this was not the case. In ancient times and in the early historical period as well, even the most densely populated towns depended on both game animals and corn. The situation is reflected in two well-remembered myths, the tale of the release of impounded game and the story of the origin of corn from the body of a woman.

Of considerable importance to the Alabama, Koasati, and Creek tribes, these myths were usually told separately, sometimes as drawn-out tales with many episodes. Among the Cherokee, however, at least one version has been recorded that combines the two stories into one. This is the myth of *Kanáti*, the lucky hunter, and the woman called *Selu* (corn).

Whenever *Kanáti* went into the woods, he never failed to bring back a load of game for his wife, *Selu*, and their little boy. The mother washed the meat at the riverside, and in time the blood rose up from the water as a second boy, called He Who Grew Up Wild. Secretly the two boys followed their father to see how he managed to get fat bucks, does, and turkeys. In the mountains, far to the west, they saw him remove a rock slab that covered the entrance to a cave. Out came one deer. A few days later the boys returned to the cave by themselves, released a deer, but were not quick enough, and in their confusion they allowed all the birds and animals to escape. Since that time the animals have been scattered in the forest, and hunting is difficult.

Now the boys were hungry, and there was no meat. Spying on

their mother, they watched her produce corn and beans from her body by rubbing her stomach and her armpits. Disgusted, they refused to eat this food when she tried to serve it to them. They feared she was a witch and planned to kill her—to which she assented, instructing them to bury her body and keep vigil overnight. They did, and the next morning corn had grown up, ready for harvest. Hearing the news, people came from far away to ask for corn. The boys gave them some but warned them to keep vigil each night of their seven days' journey back home. On the seventh night, though they tried to stay awake, the people could not help sleeping, and for this reason corn does not mature rapidly, and farming is hard work.

In the Creek, Alabama, and Koasati versions the father turns into a crow, suggesting the Plains myths in which Crow is the master of impounded game. The story of corn produced from the body of a spirit is virtually absent from the Plains but is widespread in the East and Midwest. In a version recorded among the Wabanaki of New England the corn tassels are yellow because the woman is fair-haired. In an Iroquois variant the corn stalks grow from the woman's breasts. The Chippewa are unusual (though not unique) in having the plant spring from the body of the male corn spirit, *Mondamin.* A rare Plains occurrence has been reported from among the Arikara, who formerly had at least one story in which Mother Corn is killed while visiting her people. From her body spring various crops.

Folkloristically, the story of the lucky hunter and the corn mother is close to the Plains tale of Lodge Boy and Thrown Away. This can be seen more clearly in a Creek version, where the second boy is born from the afterbirth tossed aside after the mother has been killed by a monster and the first child has been delivered safely.

Rabbit

The figure of Br'er Rabbit, the South's best-known contribution to world folklore, can be traced to both North American and African sources. Since each of the two continents counts the rabbit trickster among its own traditions, the untangling of influences in the Southeast has been a subject of long-standing debate. Undoubtedly Indians and Black Africans traded Rabbit tales. The question is how much, and in which direction.

Although Rabbit is hardly a culture hero for Southeastern Indians, he does play the leading role in The Theft of Fire. There was fire in the "big house" only, according to a Yuchi variant. At a dance there, Rabbit was asked to be the leader. He put tar on his hands, and while making gestures to lead the dance, he swatted the fire so that the coals stuck to his hands. Off he ran with the coals, chased by the owners. They caused rain to fall, but Rabbit took refuge in a hollow log. When the rain stopped, he set fire to the ground. Then the people gathered up the burning wood that lay everywhere and went home with it. In this way they got their fire.

Presumably Indian, the story nevertheless has a point in common with the famous Br'er Rabbit and the Tar Baby. In that tale, presumably African, the trickster himself is tricked when he swats at a doll made of tar and sticks fast.

An unusual Alabama variant has Rabbit stealing not fire but the sun. An old woman, it seems, kept the sun in a pot. Rabbit went to a dance at her house, danced near the pot, and stole it when she wasn't looking. After the usual chase, he breaks the pot. Then all the other animals help him place the sun in the sky.

The Creation

Cooperation among animals—the council-of-animals theme—recurs in major creation myths of the Cherokee, Yuchi, and other tribes. According to a nineteenth-century Cherokee account, all the animals were originally in *galúnlati,* the world above the sky vault, which is made of solid rock. Beneath, there was nothing but water.

Since the animals were crowded in *galúnlati,* they wondered if there could be anything under the water. At last the water beetle, called Beaver's Grandchild, offered to go find out. It dived to the bottom and came up with soft mud, which grew until it formed the island we call earth.

At first the earth was soft and wet, too soft for the animals to come down. They kept sending birds to fly over it to see if it was dry. When the buzzard flew over, he got tired and began to flap his wings, pressing down valleys and lifting up mountains in the soft earth. When the world finally dried, the animals descended. And as heavenly bodies, plants, and human beings were gradually established, the myth age came to a close.

In a Chitimacha version the earth diver and the creation of heavenly bodies and human beings are directed by the supreme spirit, Thoumé, who has neither eyes nor ears, yet sees and knows everything. From his body he derived the beginnings of all life.

In Yuchi belief the animal people originally lived in *yubahé* (far heights). Even Sun and Moon had animal form in those days, and everyone would get together at the rainbow for dances and ceremonies. With the decision to create earth, the myth age came to a close.

According to one of the fullest of the Yuchi versions, Sun herself directed the animals in the initial act of creation. First she asked Beaver to dive for mud, then Fish Otter, then Crawfish. Crawfish succeeded, and the earth was made. Next, various animals took turns trying to light the world, first Glowworm, then Star, then Moon. But none had sufficient light. Sun made the final attempt and succeeded. When she got to the top of the sky, however, she wasn't sure whether to continue downward to the west. Should there be perpetual day, or should there be night?

After some debate the animals decided in favor of night, as providing the only proper time for sexual relations. Here again we have the regulation of day and night, one of the great themes in Indian mythology.

The female sun

The sun's preeminence in Southeast lore is unmistakable, especially in the older traditions. Often as not, and perhaps typically, the sun was a woman. In eighteenth-century reports on the Tunica, who were neighbors of the Natchez, the sun is listed first among the various deities, and it is said—mysteriously—that the two household gods of the Tunica were "a toad and a figure of a woman, which they worshipped, believing that these represented the sun."

In the 1930s it was possible to collect a fragmentary solar myth from the last surviving Tunica speaker, Sesostrie Youchigant of Avoyelles Parish, Louisiana. In Youchigant's story, a variant of The Disappointed Bride, a young woman whose kingfisher husband brings her nothing but minnows escapes to the sky, becoming the sun. Whether the myth was current in the eighteenth century, or was adopted later, cannot be known for sure.

In Yuchi mythology the sun is male if it is the culture hero, female if it is the Creator. According to the usual story, the Yuchi were born from menstrual blood dropped by the sun as she traveled across the sky.

In an unusual Orpheus myth recorded among the Cherokee, the people of the ancient time are said to have tried to kill the sun because her rays were too hot. By mistake her daughter was killed instead, and the grief-stricken sun stayed in her house, causing darkness. In hopes of restoring the light, people traveled to the dead land and started carrying the daughter back in a box, not to be opened until they reached home. But before the time was up, they gave in to the young woman's plea for air, opened the box, and watched her fly off as a cardinal. From this we know that the cardinal is the daughter of the sun. And if the people had obeyed instructions, there would have been no permanent death, as there is now.

Nani Waiya

Emergence stories provide another distinctly female element in the oral literature of the Southeast. According to the Choctaw, the various tribes emerged in the ancient days from their "mother," *Nani Waiya,* a hill that has been located in Winston

County, Mississippi, near the headwaters of the Pearl River. Supposedly there is, or was, an open shaft leading from the underworld to the summit of this hill. In some versions the people emerge in company with grasshoppers. Others say that, after emerging, the people rested on the slopes until their bodies became dry.

During the Removal era of the 1830s many Choctaw refused to emigrate, saying that they could not leave their mother. Today more than four thousand of their descendants still live in east central Mississippi, in the vicinity of *Nani Waiya*. They are one of the largest Indian groups left in the south, and most continue to speak their native language.

Seventeen ◁

The Northeast:
Turtle Island

Ancestors' voices

As in pre-Columbian times, the Iroquois of New York still make and use ceremonial rattles fashioned from dried, whole turtle shells. So important is the turtle in Iroquois lore that in 1977 the Native American Center at Lewiston, New York, took the unusual step of announcing plans for a new headquarters to be built in the shape of a turtle, with four legs and a tail, the mouth to be used as the main entrance.

For the Iroquois, the turtle represents the earth itself and symbolizes the people's kinship with the natural world. In their version of The Earth Diver, the mud brought up from the bottom of the primeval sea was spread over the turtle's back—on which the world island still rests.

The concept of the earth as a turtle island once extended to the Iroquois' close relatives, the Huron, and to their Algonkian neighbors on either side, the Delaware and the Shawnee. Farther west it has persisted as a minor motif in the lore of the Chippewa, the Mandan, the Gros Ventre, and even the Arapaho of Colorado. Except for the Mandan, these western tribes are Algonkian speakers, who may have brought the idea with them when they pushed into the Plains.

In the old turtle-island country only the six nations of the Iroquois—Mohawk, Oneida, Onondaga, Cayuga, Seneca, and Tuscarora—remain in force. Huron, Delaware, and Shawnee communities survive in scattered locations, particularly in Oklahoma, while others, including the Mahican and the Nanticoke, have all but lost their cultural identity.

The vitality of the modern Iroquois may be explained in part by their strong political presence, going back to the great days of the Iroquois League, which was functioning effectively as early as the late 1600s. Today many of the ancient traditions are alive, notably the music, the political ceremonialism, and the languages.

Mythology, perhaps, has fared less well, though it must be kept in mind that the Iroquois no longer share their traditional lore as freely as they used to. In the 1980s, for example, many Iroquois believed that photographs of the False Faces, or masks used in healing ceremonies, should not be reproduced. But it is all right to publish drawings or paintings of the Faces. In 1978 I asked a Seneca singer for permission to include one of his songs in a phonograph album. To take just one "wouldn't hurt anybody," he explained, but if I had asked for an entire song cycle the answer would have been no.

A book of myths and tales published by Mohawks in 1976 includes very little that can be compared to the important Iroquois myth collections made around the turn of the century. No doubt the art of mythmaking has declined. Yet the book opens with an oration in the Mohawk language that includes this ringing phrase: Onkwehshón: 'a shé:kon ionkwahronkhátie' ionkhihso-thokon'kénha' ra'otiwén:na' (People, we are still constantly hearing our ancestors' voices).

The Woman Who Fell from the Sky

The two most successful collectors of Iroquois mythology were themselves part Iroquois: J. N. B. Hewitt (1859–1937), of Tuscarora descent, and Arthur C. Parker (1881–1955), whose English surname has been carried by prominent Senecas since the early 1800s. Hewitt, who had access to an older generation of narrators, made the Creation myth his specialty, filing monumental Onondaga, Mohawk, and Seneca versions with the Bureau of Ethnology in Washington.

Hewitt preferred to call this myth the Iroquoian "cosmology." Folklorists know it as The Woman Who Fell from the Sky. In its all-inclusiveness it ranks with the fullest of the Southwest Emergence myths, its scope limited only by the narrator's knowledge and by the time allotted for the telling of it. The Creation, the origin of human livelihood, and the deeds of the culture hero are its main themes.

Invariably the opening scene is set in the world above the sky vault, where a young woman becomes the bride of a man usually portrayed as much older. Although the subject is handled with delicacy, one supposes that the husband may be his wife's father or even her brother. In some versions, when the woman becomes pregnant, her husband suspects her of adultery.

As a result of her sexual transgression, real or imagined, the

---

The Woman Who Fell from the Sky. The ducks that will cushion her fall and the turtle whose back will form the earth are shown in this 1946 watercolor entitled *Creation Legend,* by Tom Dorsey, Onondaga. Philbrook Art Center, Tulsa, Oklahoma.

tree of life in the sky world is uprooted and the pregnant woman flung downward through the opening. As she falls, ducks flock under her to cushion her descent, bringing her safely to the water that lies below. Then, to make her a permanent resting place, the assembled animals agree that the muskrat will dive for earth.

The bottom is so deep that by the time the muskrat resurfaces he is dead. But in his claws and mouth the beaver finds plenty of earth, which the turtle volunteers to support. As the earth increases, the turtle also grows larger until the world reaches its proper size. At precisely that moment the fallen woman gives birth to a daughter.

In time the daughter matures and is impregnated by Wind or by a mysterious stranger who merely lays an arrow beside her and departs. In the most elegant of all the versions, narrated by Chief John Arthur Gibson in 1900, the stranger deposits two arrows, one untipped (which he scrupulously straightens), the other flint-tipped. The result is that the daughter gives birth to twin boys, the first of whom is the culture hero, called Sapling, the Good Mind, or *Teharonhyawágon* (holder of the heavens). The second, who is Flint or the Evil Mind, comes into the world through his mother's armpit, killing her in the process. The fallen woman, now the grandmother, becomes the twins' guardian.

From this point on, the story varies considerably from teller to teller. In general the acts of creation are performed by Sapling, who tries to fashion an ideal world. Flint, aided by the grandmother, does whatever he can to undo the work, making life difficult for human beings.

It is said that wherever Sapling ran, maple seedlings sprang up behind him; and whenever he threw a handful of earth, living things flew off in all directions. The animals that Sapling created were impounded in a cave by Flint, but Sapling released them. Flint began building an ice bridge across the water so that monsters could cross over and eat humans. But Sapling sent the bluebird to frighten Flint, and the ice melted. Such stories are regarded by the Iroquois as allegories of winter and spring. The impoundment of the animals represents hibernation.

The grandmother made the sun out of her dead daughter's

head and with Flint's help hid it far to the east. Sapling, assisted by animals, stole it and fastened it to the sky.

Sapling made two-way rivers for easy canoe travel. But Flint undid the work, causing rivers to flow in one direction only.

Eventually Sapling retires from the earth, first killing or banishing Flint, who in some versions becomes the master of the underworld. According to Chief Gibson, the "three sisters"—corn, beans, and squash—grow up from Sapling's buried corpse as his spirit walks into the sky. (According to other accounts, the "sisters" spring from the body of his mother.)

Like other North American heroes, Sapling, despite his importance in myth, is not the subject of old-style rituals. However, in the modern religion of the Seneca, which has spread throughout Iroquoia, Sapling is identified with the Master of Life, the usual recipient of prayers. This partially integrated approach to ritual and mythology, incorporating ideas from Quaker missionaries, dates from the teachings of Handsome Lake, the Seneca prophet who revitalized Iroquois religion during the period 1799–1815.

The council style

Oratory in the grand manner, worthy of the courtroom or the legislative chamber, appears to have been a specialty of the central-eastern and midwest tribes, whether Iroquoian, Algonkian, or Siouan. The secular tone and the carefully balanced phrases set the style even for sacred rituals like the Delaware Big House Ceremony, the Winnebago Medicine Rite, Fox bundle ceremonies, and Iroquois mourning councils.

Occasionally the council style spills over into myth recitals, of which the following passage from Chief Gibson's Creation epic may be taken as an example. Here the culture hero, having made the first man, turns to the task of creating woman.

"Now at that time he made another. As to that one, too, he made her flesh from the earth. And when he had completed it he said, 'That, perhaps, will result in good that I make them alike. That one, too, shall be like me in my bodily movements.' Then at that time he took a portion of his own life and he placed it in the body of her whom he had just made; also he took a portion of his mind and placed it in the head of her whose body he had just finished; also he took a portion of his blood and placed it in the flesh of her whose body he had just finished. Then at that time he took a portion of his power to look around and to talk and placed them both in her head which was part of her body. Then he put his breath into her body as a part of it. So now verily she came to life."

The Shawnee female deity

Reports by early travelers and missionaries indicate that The Woman Who Fell from the Sky was the principal myth not only of the Iroquois but of the Huron, the Shawnee, probably the Delaware, and perhaps the Mahican, another Algonkian tribe, formerly of the Hudson Valley. As late as 1900 the story still survived in great detail among the Wyandot, a division of the Huron that had moved westward in the seventeenth century, finally settling in Kansas and Oklahoma.

In the older Huron versions, collected by French Jesuits in Canada, the fallen woman is called *Yatahéntshi* (ancient body) and the culture hero is *Yuskeha*. These texts vary considerably, perhaps because each clan had its own lore—evidently a factor in all the mythologies of the lower Northeast except the Iroquois. In a few of the Huron variants *Yatahéntshi* is portrayed as both the mother of humanity and the keeper of the dead, taking the place of the evil twin of the Iroquois versions. Her grandson, *Yuskeha*, governs the fate of the living.

In Shawnee variants the fallen woman rises to even greater prominence, assuming the role of Creator. Known as Cloud or Our Grandmother, she descended from the sky and created the turtle, the earth, and the features of earth and sky. Her grandson, Cloudy Boy, and his little dog traveled with her.

Against the Creator's wishes, Cloudy Boy killed a huge man by knifing him in the stomach, and from the wound poured a flood that covered the world. Our Grandmother then remade the land, using the crawfish as her earth diver. In time she created the Shawnee, showed them how to raise corn, how to hunt, how to build houses, and how to conduct ceremonies. Her duties accomplished, she withdrew to the sky.

The influence of this female deity in Shawnee lore no doubt derives from the profound reverence for motherhood that characterized all the cultures of the East, west of New England, where clan names were handed down from mother to child and women were regarded as founders of nations. In this connection it may be mentioned that emergence themes are also to be found in the Shawnee-Huron-Iroquois area, just as they are in the Southeast. Among many of the tribes, however, the emergence tends to be an incidental or optional feature of the mythology, especially in the north.

Shorter myths

In the art of fiction the Iroquois rival the Pueblos and the Eskimo, displaying a fondness for purely fictional tales that have little to do with either myth or folklore. In general, the Creation epic comprises Iroquois myth, just as the Emergence cycle expands to contain virtually all mythic themes for the Zuni. The rest, by contrast, has a secular flavor.

Nevertheless, there are occasional items of mythic interest among the shorter tales, and these help give a fuller picture of Northeast mythology, revealing links to neighboring regions, particularly the Southeast.

The Hungry Pleiades. In the Old World as well as the New, and in both northern and southern hemispheres, the annual reappearance of the seven stars, or Pleiades, is thought to signal the beginning or the end of the season of plenty. For the Indians of North America the Pleiades are a winter constellation, associated with food shortages and desperate hunters.

According to an Iroquois version, there once were seven children who loved to dance, despite their disapproving mothers, who withheld food. Hungry, the children became light-headed, and as they continued their dancing they rose into the air, becoming the familiar constellation. With respect to the seventh, barely visible, star, it is said that one of the children, who looked down and therefore fell back to earth, grew up as a pine—which is felt to be related to starlight on account of the latent fire in pitchwood.

The Cherokee of North Carolina have the same story. But according to a Natchez variant, the stars in question were once seven people who fasted in the woods to gain the gift of prophecy. They stayed away so long that they felt it was too late to return home, and they changed themselves into pines. It is said that when the Europeans came and chopped down the forests, the seven escaped to the sky, becoming the Pleiades.

The Sky Maidens. One of the world's most widespread folktales —in the opinion of some folklorists, at least—is the so-called Swan Maidens, the story of a man who marries one of several bird women who eventually reverts to bird form and flies away. It is doubtful, however, that the numerous Eurasian, African, and American tales grouped under this heading are truly related. The North American Indian representative is a continent-wide Canadian and arctic tale in which the heroine is a goose woman who flies off after having two children with her human husband. Within the Iroquois sphere of influence and in the Southeast, where the story does not occur, it is replaced by a somewhat more mythic tale that will here be called The Sky Maidens.

In a well-known Shawnee variant, collected in the early 1800s, the hero is White Hawk, a hunter, who observes twelve shining maidens descending to earth in a basket. The maidens dance in a clearing, circling around a bright ball. Before they can withdraw to the sky, however, White Hawk captures the youngest. He makes her his wife, and she bears him a son. Yet she secretly weaves a new basket, and when it is ready, she and her child get into it and rise to the sky, where they are greeted by her people, the stars.

Because the little boy misses his father, the star chief orders his daughter to return to earth, telling her to have her husband bring back a specimen of every kind of animal he has killed in his hunting. This the young man does, carrying wings, claws, and feet up to the sky world. The stars then gather around the gifts, each becoming the bird or animal it chooses. The hunter, his wife, and their son become white hawks, and all the newly formed animals descend from the sky, spreading out over the earth.

Thunder and Serpent. Thunder spirits and water monsters inhabit the lore of most Indian cultures. But nowhere do they occur so persistently in combination as in the tales of the Iroquoian-speaking tribes, which include the Huron-Wyandot and the distantly related Cherokee. In keeping with the Iroquoian love of allegory, these myths represent the perennial struggle between good and evil, with thunder triumphing over the dangerous serpent. A favorite Iroquois treatment has thunder, or a band of thunderers, rescuing a maiden who has been abducted by the serpent. (Such stories extend westward, with good examples recorded among the Menominee of Wisconsin.) Publishing a Cherokee story on the same theme, the Kilpatricks call it "the noblest, most moving myth that we heard in our collecting travels."

The Cherokee tale, however, dispenses with the maiden. Instead, we have two boys who find a snake in the woods and agree to bring it food in exchange for the promise that it will be their helper. Thus fed, it grows to enormous size, sprouting horns. One day the boys find it locked in combat with Thunder, who pleads for their aid, promising to help them always. Faced with the choice, the boys side with Thunder and shoot the serpent dead. "That's why Thunder is with us as long as we live," comments the narrator. "God made it that way: that Lightning-and-Thunder and human beings should live together."

The roots of peace

Tree symbolism, associated with Old World myths and prominent in the lore of South America, is perhaps more fully developed in the lower Northeast region than in any other part of North America. In The Woman Who Fell from the Sky, the tree that grows in the upper world commands attention either for its year-round supply of fruit or as a source of light in place of the sun. In a Mohawk version, the light radiates from the tree's large white flowers, said to be dogwood blossoms.

In an old Delaware story, the tree grew from the turtle's back, not in the sky world but here on earth, and the first humans were produced from its branches. As a philosophical concept, referred to in ritual rather than in myth, the Seneca envision a world tree whose branches pierce the sky and whose roots extend to the waters of the underworld. Accordingly, in their curing ceremonies the Seneca False Faces rub their turtle rattles on pine-tree trunks to obtain sky power and earth power.

The Great League, or Peace, of the Iroquois is itself symbolized by an enormous tree, supposed to have been planted by the League's founder, *Deganawida.* The event occurred not in mythic times but, as many believe, only a generation before the arrival of the Europeans. According to the various legends, *Deganawida* was born to a Huron virgin; he matured rapidly, then crossed Lake Ontario in a white stone canoe to reform the warring Iroquois, who lived to the south.

In Mohawk country, *Deganawida* met the warrior Hiawatha, said to have been a cannibal. Under *Deganawida*'s influence, Hiawatha changed his ways and began to help form the League. Soon the Oneida, the Cayuga, and the Seneca were joined with the Mohawk. But the Onondaga, controlled by the evil chief, *Atotarho,* held out. At last Hiawatha "combed the snakes" from *Atotarho*'s "hair," and the Onondaga fell in line.

Planting the tree of peace, *Deganawida* announced that "four great, long, white roots" would shoot out to the four directions to guide the people to the shade of the tree, while an eagle would perch at the summit to warn the nations in case of outside attack.

Among the several tree symbols bequeathed to them by their traditional lore, the twentieth-century Iroquois—with increasing political awareness—have chosen to emphasize this tree of *Deganawida.* Together with the turtle, symbol of the earth, the tree of peace has become a principal emblem of the modern Iroquois nations.

Eighteen

The Northeast: Gluskap's Country

The great liar

Unlike their neighbors to the west and south, the peoples of the upper Northeast had no creation epic. In this damp, chilly country of hunters and fishermen, Earth Diver and emergence myths were all but unheard of. Although a number of tales—including corn mother stories—passed freely up the coast, the mythology of the upper region centered around a culture hero who had as much in common with the Transformer of the Northwest Coast as with the heroes of adjacent Huron and Iroquois tribes.

For the Wabanaki-speaking groups of New England and the

Maritime Provinces of Canada, this hero was *Glúskap,* to use a
Maliseet form of the name, which varied from Micmac *Kulóskap*
to Penobscot *Gluskabé* to Abenaki *Gluskobá.* The word means
"liar," some say, because *Glúskap* deceived his enemies.

Usually he was portrayed as the principal member of a family
that included a grandmother and a younger brother. According
to a Micmac account, the old woman, in the classic manner of
earth mothers, continually rejuvenated herself. The brother,
sometimes just a little boy, called Sable or Marten, was at other
times a twin, called Wolf, and in several versions he tried to spoil
his elder brother's work, as did the Iroquois antihero, Flint.

Glúskap had no beginning. He was always there. Or, as some
tribes believed, he arrived from across the ocean and began traveling up the St. John, the St. Lawrence, or the Penobscot River.
The river journey theme recalls the Northwest Coast and Plateau
Transformer myths, as do the numerous episodes in which *Glúskap* slays monsters and reduces dangerous, gigantic animals to
proper size.

In a Penobscot story the hero freed all the hares of the world
after fighting his way through blizzards. Formerly the hares had
been people, whose brains had been combed out by a witch, who
had sent them to live with the Great White Hare. Insulated from
the outside world by a wall of snowstorms, the Great Hare had
made the hare people his prisoners. But when *Glúskap* killed their
master, the hares ran over the earth and became food for humans.

A myth that is even more typical of the region concerns a
monster frog who drank the world's water, causing a drought. By
killing the frog, *Glúskap* released the waters and so saved the
people. According to the Penobscot, various clans, or family
groups, were established at this time, when thirsty people jumped
into the newly released waters and turned into lobsters, eels,
frogs, and other water animals—founding the family groups
called Lobster, Eel, and so forth.

In other adventures, *Glúskap* outwits the amorous but evil Jug
Woman, rescues his brother from the serpent *Atosis,* and tames
the wind bird.

For many he was the great teacher, said to have taught hunting
and farming and to have given names to the stars. Among the

Passamaquoddy he was known for at least a few acts of creation; it was believed that he had shot arrows into an ash tree, and people had come out of the bark. He had also created animals, some too large, like the squirrel, which he reduced by smoothing it down with his hands.

In late, Christianized myths from the western Wabanaki, *Glúskap* even created himself, rising out of the dust left over from the creation of Adam. By the twentieth century the Abenaki knew the hero only as *Odzihózo* (he makes himself from something), the old name *Gluskobá* having faded from memory.

Djokábesh

From a historian's point of view the *Glúskap* cycle has had a lamentably short existence. None of it was recorded until the 1870s, and in less than a hundred years it had ceased to be a vital element in Wabanaki culture. By contrast, the *Djokábesh* cycle of the Montagnais and Naskapi, whose homeland lies north of the Wabanaki, has been known to the outside world for three hundred and fifty years. As collected by Père Paul Le Jeune, it first appears in the *Jesuit Relations* for 1634. In 1979 it reappears—and once again in French—in a classic version translated from the Montagnais language as dictated by Francois Bellefleur of Romaine, Quebec.

Djokábesh is a transformer and monster slayer, who returns to his sister after each adventure. She warns him not to go out again but cannot help describing the perils that lie ahead. *Djokábesh* always answers, "Enough, sister. Your words frighten me. Stop terrifying me with this story." Then, telling her he is going squirrel hunting, he goes off to meet the next danger. He kills the monster bear who had eaten his mother, kills a cannibal woman (and brings home her two daughters), and is swallowed by a fish (and rescued by his sister). He also serves as the protagonist in the widespread Sun Snarer myth, in which a hero captures the too hot sun and, in some versions, succeeds in regulating its warmth.

Although many of his exploits seem to serve his own ends rather than the interests of humanity, *Djokábesh* is regarded by the

Montagnais as a true culture hero, and myths about him are still told as *atenogan* (sacred stories).

Eastern tricksters

The mythology of the East differs from that of the Midwest, northern Plains, and Far West in assigning the trickster a decidedly inferior role. Nowhere in the Southeast or Northeast does the trickster rise to the full status of culture hero, and his participation in the great events of the ancient time is minimal at best.

Aside from the rabbit of Southeast lore, the Montagnais-Naskapi *Mésho* is perhaps the most significant of the lot—and even he may be an import from the Midwest, since both his name and his typical adventures suggest *Manabózho,* the trickster-hero of the Chippewa and other Ojibwa tribes.

In one of the most ribald of Earth Diver myths, *Mésho,* after a string of sexual and gluttonizing exploits, sends Mink beneath the flood waters to bring up soil. When Mink returns, half drowned, with a bit of mud stuck in his craw, *Mésho* revives him by artificial respiration applied to the anus—which has the effect of dislodging the mud and conveniently expanding it to form the earth.

The Montaignais-Naskapi ascribe a number of *Mésho*'s doings to Wolverine, who is also a trickster in Wabanaki lore—called *Lox* by the Maliseet-Passamaquoddy. Other Wabanaki and Iroquoian tricksters include Raccoon, Fox, Hare, Badger, and Turtle.

Little people

The contest between small and large, or, to a lesser extent, between clever and stupid, is one of the recurring themes in Indian mythology. Heroes, if they are abnormal in size, are frequently elfin, whereas villains tend to be giants, preferably stupid ones.

Rarely thumb-sized, as in European lore, the little people are generally thought to range in height from about ten inches to three feet. Although some are mischievous, as a class they are helpful, impressively clever, and sometimes quite old. According to the Wyandot, they are old enough to remember the Flood, and the Passamaquoddy believe they were here before *Glúskap.*

In northwest California the *woge,* or immortals, of the Yurok Indians are held to be little people. So are the twin war gods of the Pueblos of New Mexico. And the culture hero *Djokábesh* falls in the same category. Although *Djokábesh* matured, he never grew larger than a toddling child.

The Wabanaki and the Iroquoians do not claim diminutiveness for their culture heroes. Yet their mythologies are by no means lacking in elves. The Dark Dance, still performed by the Seneca of western New York, is a tribute to the little people in exchange for the hospitality they once showed a young Seneca man who visited their rocky dens.

In a modern Mohawk folktale, unrelated to the Dark Dance, a girl shares her picnic of corn bread and apples with a tiny family that invites her to their home inside a rock. There they feed her soup from a pot that magically refills, and they invite her to make three wishes. Her first wish is for a magic soup pot of her own so that her family will never be hungry; her second and third are for the gifts of tact and kindheartedness. The fairies comply, promising, "You will be happy and your luck will be good."

The Wabanaki, as do the Iroquois, recognize several varieties of little people, notably the *kiwalatamosísuk,* who have the gift of prophecy, and the *lumpegwenosísuk,* who live in water and inspire amorous adventures. Like the Iroquois elves, the *lumpegwenosísuk* keep magic soup pots, and it has even been said that they can make bread out of snow.

Writing recently about Micmac little people called *pukalutumush,* the anthropologist Philip Bock notes that these are "dwarf-like creatures who are believed to dress and act like 'old time Indians,' eating only wild meat and helping or harming men according to their whim. Of late they have acquired some characteristics of the French Canadian *lutins,* playing tricks around the house or barn such as riding horses at night and leaving their tails or manes tightly braided. In this manifestation, they may be exorcised with holy water or fronds from Palm Sunday."

Part Eight ↘

MIDWEST

Nineteen

The Hare Cycle

Trickster-creator-deliverer

Moving into the Great Lakes country and the upper Mississippi basin, we leave behind the dignified culture heroes of the Northeast and encounter once again the trickster-hero typical of the West. For the midwestern Siouans—the Winnebago, the Iowa, the Oto, the Omaha, the Ponca—this figure is Hare, called *Mast-shíngke* (rabbit) in the language of the Omaha. The Algonkian Ojibwa and Menominee call him *Manabózho,* or *Nánabush,* a variable name that has been translated Great Hare. According to the Menominee, he was born as a little white rabbit with quivering ears, causing his grandmother to exclaim, "Oh, my dear little rabbit, my *Mánabush!*"

However, for the other Algonkian tribes in the region, including the Cree, the Fox, the Sauk, the Kickapoo, and the Potawatomi, the hero is *Wísaka,* or *Wísakedjak* (anglicized as Whiskey Jack), not identified with the hare or with any other animal in particular. Nevertheless, *Wísakedjak* myths are variations on those told of *Manabózho.*

In general, the Siouans deemphasize the hero's trickster aspect, relegating the coarser and more trivial tales to *Ishjinki,* who corresponds to the *Inktomi* of the Sioux proper. Food production results from ribald adventures of *Ishjinki,* whereas the Siouan Rabbit is a deliverer, if a lighthearted one, rescuing humanity from the cannibal bears, bodiless heads, giants, and swallowing monsters of the ancient time. *Manabózho* and *Wísakedjak* perform similar duties but are trickster-providers and even creators as well.

Today this sacred lore, largely forgotten, is best preserved in the far north, especially among the Cree, where Hoodwinked Dancers, Eye Juggler, and similar animal tales are still told of *Wísakedjak.* Although hunting is losing out to wage occupations, and many now rely on government welfare, the Cree still think of themselves as hunters, and it is said that telling stories about animals is part of the "old agreement." If game animals know that the myths are not being kept up, they will leave.

A more worldly approach to mythology has been taken by the Cree on the Rocky Boy Reservation in northern Montana, where schoolchildren in the 1970s began learning *Wísakedjak* stories from textbooks printed in Cree syllabic writing. Before they can enter the curriculum, the tales must pass a Cree review board to make sure they have a moral ending and a strong message.

The Rolling Head

Among the Algonkians the trickster tales concerning *Manabózho-Wísakedjak* are often told separately from the more serious epic

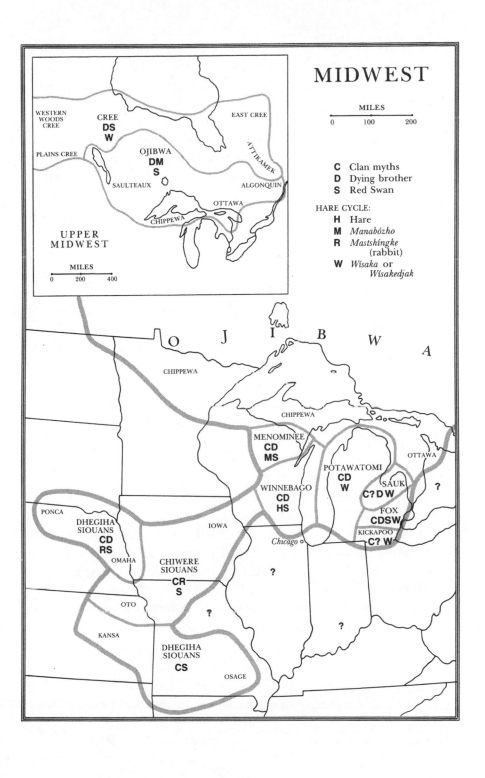

MIDWEST

MILES
0   100   200

C Clan myths
D Dying brother
S Red Swan

HARE CYCLE:
H Hare
M *Manabózho*
R *Mastshíngke*
   (rabbit)
W *Wísaka* or
   Wisakedjak

UPPER MIDWEST

MILES
0   200   400

WESTERN
WOODS
CREE

CREE
**DS
W**

EAST CREE

PLAINS CREE

OJIBWA
**DM
S**

ATTIKAMEK

SAULTEAUX

ALGONQUIN

OTTAWA

CHIPPEWA

O   J   I   B   W   A

CHIPPEWA

CHIPPEWA

MENOMINEE
**CD
MS**

OTTAWA

POTAWATOMI
**CD
W**

SAUK
C?DW

WINNEBAGO
**CD
HS**

FOX
CDSW

PONCA

DHEGIHA
SIOUANS
**CD
RS**

IOWA

KICKAPOO
C?W

Chicago

OMAHA

CHIWERE
SIOUANS
**CR
S**

?

OTO

?

?

KANSA

DHEGIHA
SIOUANS
CS

OSAGE

that relates the hero's birth, his childhood, the agonizing death of his brother, the ensuing flood, and the creation of a new earth. For the Plains Cree this epic begins with an adaptation of the widespread folktale known as The Rolling Head.

Long ago—as told in a classic version collected in 1925—a woman living alone with her husband gave birth to two sons, the first of whom was *Wisakedjak*. All went well until the husband discovered that his wife was slipping into the woods and allowing snakes to satisfy her amorous desires, "climbing this way and that all over her body."

Without the mother's knowledge, the man told his two sons to run away. Secretly he killed the snakes. He humiliated the woman by feeding her their blood, then chopped off her head and fled into the sky, saying, "Now, off in the future time man will grow into being; 'the Great Star,' they will say. That will be I."

In a fury the wife sent her buttocks after her husband, while her head rolled in pursuit of the two boys. Catching up to the children, she called out, treacherously, saying she wanted to suckle the little brother, but they ran on. Reaching a river, they were saved by a crane, who ferried them across. The crane then ferried the mother but dropped her into the water, saying, "There, in the future time man will come into being; 'Sturgeon' they will call you."

After comforting the younger brother, who cried at the loss of his mother, *Wisakedjak* abandoned him and set off on a series of monster-slaying adventures. The little brother meanwhile, in his loneliness, turned into a wolf and fell into the clutches of water serpents, who killed and skinned him and used his hide as a door flap. Hearing of this outrage, *Wisakedjak* forced his way into the serpents' den and killed their chief. In retaliation the serpents caused a world flood, from which the hero saved himself by climbing onto a raft. When the waters had stopped rising, he sent the

---

The two boys and their father are shown with their mother's head in this 1971 silk-screen print, *Legend of the Rolling Head,* by Daphne Odjig, Ottawa. John Anson Warner collection.

loon to dive for earth and so built a new world. Thus the age of animals came to a close, and the time of humans began.

The Red Swan

South of the Cree, the Ojibwa and the Menominee tell more or less the same epic cycle of the culture hero and his wolf brother. But the hero, who is now *Manabózho,* has an entirely different origin. Here it is said that he was the child of a virgin, who died giving birth, whereupon he was raised by his grandmother, sometimes identified as the earth.

Among the Winnebago, the northernmost of the Siouans, the old Hare cycle also began with the virgin birth, immediately taking up the theme of the hero who lives with his grandmother, returning to her after each escapade. Some of the adventures parallel those of *Wísakedjak* and *Manabózho;* others suggest close links with the Rabbit cycle of the Omaha. Of particular significance is Hare's culminating exploit, which follows the story line of one of the most characteristic of Midwest myths, told by Algonkians and Siouans alike, but never as part of the Hare cycle—except with the Winnebago.

Summoned to the lodge of an old, formerly redheaded man, who had lost his scalp, Hare was fed from a magically replenishing pot and sent across the wide water to retrieve the missing red hairpiece. Returning in triumph, he handed the scalp to the old man, who put it on and became young again. As his reward, Hare received a beautiful woman, who "was lying in the midst of white feathers and the only dark thing were her eyes." This woman controlled the magic pot of food. The old man had warned Hare not to take her as his wife. But the hero could not resist, and as he broke the prohibition the magic food—which would otherwise have been available forever—disappeared. Because of Hare's sin, it became necessary for humans to work for their livelihood.

In a Menominee variant, which follows the more usual pattern, the colors are reversed: the scalp is white, and the bird woman is red. Again she is red, brilliantly red, in the earliest recorded version of the story, the Ojibwa myth called The Red Swan, collected by Schoolcraft in the 1830s.

Twins

A basic difference between the Siouan Rabbit, or Hare, cycles and those of the Algonkian tribes has to do with the figure of the younger brother, whose presence in the Algonkian epics gives them an added complexity. No doubt this helps explain why the culture hero dominates the mythologies of the upper Midwest, but not of the lower region. Though he remains in touch with his grandmother, the Siouan Hare is a solitary figure.

As if to make up for the lack, the Siouan mythologies include extended sagas of nameless twin heroes, one of which is the type known as Lodge Boy and Thrown Away, already described as a major myth of the Plains region. The best Midwest examples were recorded in the early 1900s by the Winnebago specialist Paul Radin, who found them comparable to the *Iliad* and the *Odyssey* and referred to them as "prose epics."

Though in simpler form, Lodge Boy and Thrown Away was also told by the Algonkians. Characteristically, the Ojibwa treated it as a *windigo* story. That is, the monster who devoured the twins' mother was presented as a particular kind of north woods cannibal—a giant with a heart of ice—known to both the Ojibwa and the Cree as *windigo*. *Windigo* stories are still told in the north, and it is said that crazed individuals sometimes turn into these icehearted fiends and have to be cured by a dose of hot tallow. The so-called *windigo* psychosis has been the subject of continuing discussion among anthropologists, who find it as fascinating, if not more so, than do the Algonkians themselves.

The dying brother

If a single myth were to be chosen to represent the Midwest tribes, the story of the hero's reaction to the death of his brother would perhaps be the most compelling candidate. For the Sauk and the Fox of former times it can be singled out as the most sacred of stories, and for the other Algonkians, especially the Menominee and the southwestern Ojibwa, or Chippewa, its profound religious significance was beyond question.

We have already seen how the Cree cycle that began with The Rolling Head reached its climax in *Wísakedjak*'s revenge for the loss of his wolf brother. Among the Menominee the brother was called *Mokwáyo,* also identified as a wolf. The Fox and the Potawatomi named him *Chibiábos.* In Fox mythology he became the ruler of the dead, and prayers were addressed to him.

Even such minor details as the dead brother's skin being used by the serpents as a door flap was retained from tribe to tribe. In nearly every version the hero expressed his grief dramatically when the full realization of his brother's disappearance struck him. In a Fox variant he "gulped sobbing, and the earth moved and quaked." According to the Menominee, as he sighed the earth trembled, which caused hills and ridges to form on its surface.

In a few of the accounts it is obvious that this is a myth of the origin of death. But its significance is not always transparent, and the story admits varying shades of interpretation. For lack of a twin or younger brother the Siouans could not incorporate the story in their hare cycle. Instead, they told it separately, suggesting (in the case of the Winnebago) that the death was punishment for the elder brother's excessive pride, or (with the Omaha) that the separation of the two brothers brought about the origin of the Deer and Wolf clans.

Dim echoes of the story reach as far west as the Blackfeet and the Assiniboin and east to the Montagnais. The myth's curious similarity to the Great Basin story of the death of Wolf, which in turn is related to The Dying God of Arizona and southern California, may be charged to coincidence. It is worth noting that the theme of the culture hero who loses his brother is one that surfaces in widely separated mythologies—in the Kwakiutl, for example, and in the Iroquois.

The Medicine Rite

Following the "red swan" episode in the Winnebago Hare cycle, the hero arranges the hunting relationship between men and animals, in order that people will have food, and his grandmother establishes death so that the world will not become overcrowded. When he saw that his grandmother's decision was irreversible, Hare "took his blanket, covered himself with it, lay down in the corner, and wept. He wept for the people. It was at that time that he thought of creating the Medicine Rite."

The myth refers to what was once the principal Winnebago ceremony, a rite devoted to the problem of death and the mystic doctrine of reincarnation. Its central idea is dramatized by the symbolic shooting of individual participants, who then "return" to life. Presumably the Medicine Rite came from the Ojibwa, who were practicing it at least as early as the eighteenth century. Better known as the *Midéwiwin,* or Grand Medicine, it spread to all the Algonkian tribes in the region, except the Cree. Omaha, Iowa, Ponca, and Santee Sioux forms have also been reported.

Equal in status to the Sun Dance of the Plains, the Rite is the characteristic ceremony of the Midwest region. Although for most groups it is a thing of the past, it persists among the Menominee and the Chippewa, where it is recognized as the mainstay of the traditional religion.

According to the Chippewa, the Medicine Rite was given to *Manabózho* by the *mánitos,* or spirits, to console him for the death of Wolf. The Sauk, the Menominee, and other Algonkians also connect the Rite with the Hare cycle, especially with the episode of the the dying brother.

As fully told by the old-time Winnebago, the origin myth of the Rite explained how Earthmaker, after creating the earth, made Hare in the image of man. Then he sent him—his own son—to the world below, where he was born to a virgin, later founding the sacred ceremony in order to secure immortality for humans. Virtually the same story was told by the Iowa, who were strongly influenced by the Winnebago.

Christian elements may be detected in such a myth, and in fact the Winnebago who converted to the Peyote Religion around the turn of the century openly identified Hare with Christ. A less venturesome Menominee view, dating from the same period, holds that the hero was a "friend" of Christ. As for the Winnebago Earthmaker, this deity has its counterpart in the *Kitche Mánito* (great spirit), who frequently intrudes upon the Algonkian hare cycles, even those of the Cree. Although the concept of a supreme spirit probably existed in Midwest lore before European contact, it was evidently refashioned to bring the old mythology in line with the Christian ideal.

The *Walam Olum*

A Christianized and much abbreviated version of the Hare cycle has been preserved in the *Walam Olum* (red score) of the Delaware Indians, a pictographic text found in the state of Indiana and known to have existed since 1820. Because the pictographs are memory aids, not actual words, the myth cannot be fully reconstructed, even though each symbol is accompanied by explanatory phrases in the Delaware language.

The gist of the story is that the Great Spirit—as in the book of Genesis—created the earth, the sun, the stars, the water creatures, the land creatures, and the creatures of the air. People lived in contentment until things were spoiled by a "strong snake." Pictographs show a male figure (*Nánabush*?) fighting this deadly enemy. Flood waters rise, caused by the snake, and the earth is covered. Then *"Nánabush, the powerful rabbit,"* creates(?) a new earth, or "turtle," and the world is reestablished—the same story,

The Great and Mischievous Nanabush, acrylic, 1975, by Blake Debassige, Ottawa. The artist writes: "On one of his many fishing voyages, he caught a supply of whales from the big water. The weight was too much for his canoe to carry. He decided to carry his catch on his back, using the various islands as stepping stones. The painting describes both his greatness and the silliness of his human nature." McMichael Canadian Collection, Kleinburg, Ontario.

in outline form, that we have already seen in the Cree variant that begins with The Rolling Head.

Driven from New Jersey and southeastern New York, the Delaware were living in Indiana around the turn of the nineteenth century and are known to have had contact with the Chippewa, the most likely source for this standard Midwest Algonkian myth. No one knows why the Delaware recorded it. One theory is that they hoped it would validate their claim to land ownership in Indiana. If so, they were disappointed. The Delaware tribe eventually pushed on to Oklahoma, and the *Walam Olum* fell into the hands of non-Indian antiquaries.

Twenty

Lore of the Kin

World pictures

Tribes of the central and lower Midwest were divided into kinship groups, usually thought of as representing the component parts of the universe. Among the Omaha there were ten such units, five of which considered themselves "sky" clans; the other five were the "earth" clans.

The Winnebago had a similar system, recognizing four clans "above" and eight "below," each named for a particular animal. In the mind's eye these occupied five tiers: heaven of heavens (Thunderbird clan); sky (Hawk, Eagle, and Pigeon clans); earth

(Bear, Wolf, etc.); water (Fish); and subaquatic (Water Spirit).

Simultaneously and without reference to the animal levels, the Winnebago believed the universe to be made up of four superimposed worlds, the highest of which was ruled by Earthmaker. Beneath were two sky worlds, each with its presiding spirit. The fourth world was the earth itself (ruled by the culture hero, Hare), which included an underworld, governed by the evil spirit *Hereshgunina.*

In the words of the myth, Earthmaker "created a world for him[self] to sit upon and live. Then a second world he created and then a third. There were thus three worlds. Finally, he formed a fourth one, a smaller one. He made it round and after he had finished it he thrust his thumb into it, and pressed it out to prevent it from bouncing up and down and to give it the shape it now has."

But since it continued to wobble, Earthmaker placed an Island Anchorer at each of the four quarters, east, south, west, and north, and a row of four water spirits and four spirit snakes as underworld supports—so completing what German mythologists have called a *Weltbilt,* or world picture.

As a rule, intricate world pictures are found in cultures that have compartmentalized or stratified social structures. The Cree, the northernmost of the Midwest tribes, are lacking in both features. They have no clans and little or no interest in world levels and world quarters. On the whole, however, the Midwest is noteworthy for its world pictures, rivaled perhaps by the Northwest Coast and outdone only by the socially complex and highly formal Southwest.

Sky people

In most Midwest tribes each kin group had at least one narrative of its own, either a legend that explained how the clan had acquired its sacred bundle, or a myth accounting for the origin of the clan itself. Hawk, Eagle, and other bird clans were thought to have descended from the sky. Among the southern Siouans some clans traced their origins to stars that had fallen to earth.

Of the descent myths that have been preserved, the most elaborate came from the Osage, who strung them out in reiterative chants performed in clan ceremonies. The essential idea was that the ancestors had originally roamed the skies as disembodied ghosts, or "children," seeking spirit helpers who could give them human souls and human bodies. In one of the chants, after wandering upward through the four sky worlds, the children reach the female Red Bird:

> *"Ho, grandmother!*
> *The children have no bodies."*
> *She replied, "I can cause your children to have [human] bodies from my own.*
> *"My left wing shall be a left arm for the children.*
> *My right wing shall be a right arm for them.*
> *My head shall be a head for them.*
> *My mouth shall be a mouth for them."*

Another of the clans was said to have descended as eagles, alighting on a great red oak tree. The branches shuddered under their weight and dropped so many acorns that it was taken as a sign that the people would become numerous. Some of the stories told how the people, after flying to earth, got the food they needed to grow strong. An elk rolled on the bare mud, shedding hairs that sprouted beans and corn. Or a buffalo rolled over, and an ear of red corn and a red pumpkin fell from his left hind leg.

Land and water people

The Winnebago used to say that the bird clans had been the first to arrive on earth, flying down from the sky and assuming human form the instant they alighted. Then the "below" clans had emerged from the ground or come out of the water, as the case might be.

The same pattern held for other tribes in the region, though a clan's name did not always indicate if its origin myth would be of the descent or the emergence type. Some of the kin groups used deceptive nicknames, and in the more southerly tribes clan myths were influenced by general theories that favored one or the other of the two modes of origin.

The Winnebago, the Oto, and the Iowa were in agreement that the Bear clan had come out of the earth. According to a Winnebago version, the Bear ancestors emerged one by one, and as each was about to make his appearance the ground shook violently. On account of these tremors, fruits, torn loose, were scattered over the land. The Deer clan, it was said, simply appeared at the center of the earth. Appropriately, the Water Spirit ancestors emerged from a swift, deep whirlpool that carried blackened embers from underworld fires.

The linking of a food myth with the establishment of the kin recurs in an unusual Potawatomi narrative describing the early days of the Fish clan. In the beginning of the world, goes the story, a young couple lost their first child, a boy, and in their grief they went off to live by themselves. One day while the man was away hunting, his wife went down to the water's edge to wash clothes. Accidentally she caught a sunfish.

The woman was so lonely for her lost child that she played with the fish and sang to it. She made it swim, and petted it, until, behold, it turned into a human baby! She put it to her breast, and it nursed.

When the husband came, loaded with meat, they made a feast of the breast of a deer, carried it to the water, and gave it to the fishes, thanking them for sending back their child. Then they returned to their relatives and held the ceremony called *Chipá Kikwaio* (feast of the dead). Again they honored the fishes with offerings of food. Afterward, in their dreams, a trout came and told them that the Fish clan would become the greatest division of their people.

Years passed, and the fish boy grew up. In the meantime his parents had had nine other boys, but these sons were never told the strange history of their older brother. One day he said to his mother, "I would like to go hunting and take my brothers with me." His mother was pleased and told the others to obey him.

When they were a long way off in the woods, the fish boy said,

"My brothers, I am not to live on this earth always, like the rest of you. What I am about to tell you comes from the Great Spirit. Kill me, sprinkle my blood everywhere, cut off my head and throw it away. Burn my body in a brush pile. Hunt, you will have success, then go home and tell my people.

"Now, when you have done what I have told you, stay away from this place for one year. At the end of that time tell father to invite all the men to come here with him and camp. Tell mother to take tobacco and go to a certain place and pray for me. She will see corn, beans, pumpkins, and melons there. That will be me myself. Let her gather as much as she needs, and then tell her to bring the rest here to feast on me. These vegetables will be on earth with you until the last Indian."

The second half of this myth recalls the Chippewa spirit *Mondamin,* who was killed in a wrestling match and buried in the earth. From his body sprang the first corn plant. *Mondamin,* however, was not connected with a particular kin group. The Chippewa, like other Ojibwa tribes, do have clans but virtually no clan lore and no clan origin myths.

The mind of *Wakónda*

Before there were clans, the Osage, it was said, wandered from place to place in a condition known as *ganítha* (without law or order). A traditional view held that in those early days certain thinkers called Little Old Men had gathered periodically to exchange observations about the movements of heavenly bodies and to discuss the nature of the universe. In their meetings they formulated the theory that a silent, creative power fills the sky and the earth and keeps the stars, the moon, and the sun moving in perfect order. They called it *Wakónda* (mysterious power) or *Eáwawonaka* (causer of our being).

In fact this was a widespread Siouan idea, reaching as far west as the Lakota, who once believed that *Skan, Maka,* and other Lakota deities were manifestations of the Mysterious Power. *Wakónda* himself—or itself—does not normally appear in myths. Although it exercises compassion and moral judgment and can be addressed in prayer, it is never seen and does not speak.

A rare Omaha narrative connected with the Pebble Society, a secret order comparable to the Medicine Rite, explains that all things in the universe were originally "in the mind of *Wakónda.*" As the spirits in the air drew toward the earth, the primal waters miraculously evaporated. Food plants appeared, the spirits became flesh and blood, and as they began to feed, "the land vibrated with their expressions of joy and gratitude to *Wakónda.*"

In the loftiest of the Winnebago origination narratives a decidedly more active role is assigned to the Creator, whose primary faculty, nevertheless, is the power of thought. This is the often-quoted myth that opens:

"In the beginning, Earthmaker was sitting in space when he came to consciousness, and there was nothing else anywhere. He began to think of what he should do, and finally he began to cry and tears began to flow from his eyes and fall down below him. After a while he looked down below him and saw something bright. The bright objects were hidden tears that had flowed below and formed the present waters. When the tears flowed below they became the seas as they are now. Earthmaker began to think again. He thought, 'It is thus, if I wish anything; it will become as I wish, just as my tears have become seas.' Thus he thought. So he wished for light and it became light. Then he thought, 'It is as I have supposed; the things that I wished for have come into existence as I desired.' Then he again thought and wished for the earth, and this earth came into existence."

As quoted here, the text serves as a prologue to the origin myth of the Thunderbird clan, the most prominent of the Winnebago kin groups, the one from which tribal chiefs were chosen. But the story belongs properly to the lore of the Medicine Rite, which drew its members from all clans. Several versions of it have been recorded, one of which expands to accommodate the idea of the four-layered universe, providing the framework for the Winnebago world picture.

World view

With regard to clan origins, an Osage man once remarked, "We do not believe that our ancestors were really animals, birds, and so forth as told in the traditions. These things are only *wawíkuskáye* [symbols] of something higher." Saying this, he pointed to the sky. Thus the Osage story of the Red Bird whose wings, head, and mouth became the corresponding parts of humans implies symbolic kinship rather than genealogical descent.

In Winnebago myths the case seems a little different. The clan ancestor arrives on earth as an animal, immediately changing into human form. In this there is a clearer suggestion of animal ancestry, but it must be kept in mind that the animals of the myth age were animal people, not quite the familiar creatures of today. So here again the kinship is of a special kind.

For the Potawatomi Fish clan there was no real question of animal ancestry, since the fish boy was only a spiritual helper. Similar beliefs were current among the Cree and the Ojibwa, who recognized unusually powerful animals as guardian spirits, becoming affiliated with individuals, however, not with clans.

It is a truism that Indian mythology draws heavily upon theories of kinship between human and nonhuman beings, including plants and heavenly bodies as well as animals. In fact such theories are the dominant aspect of what has come to be called the world view—or worldview, as some prefer to write it—of virtually any tribal culture.

The term is an elusive one, not to be confused with "world picture," which refers to no more than a conception of how the universe is put together. More profound, "world view" expresses the manner in which the universe is thought to interact with the individual. In short, it is the individual's perception of reality. Or the term may be applied to a whole culture.

Philosophically inclined anthropologists began to speak of "world view" in the 1950s, inspired in part by earlier writings that had attempted to correlate a particular language, such as Hopi, with the thought patterns of the people who use that language. If still in need of refinement, the idea has been a powerful one because it suggests to Western civilization that there may be another kind of consciousness worth exploring.

Each Indian culture, presumably, has its own outlook on the world. But there is a recurring theme that may be described as a sense of unity, or wholeness. People in tribal cultures, we are told, tend to identify the past with the present and to blur the distinctions between space and time, the real and the imagined, and, of course, the human and the nonhuman. We are given to understand that myths, though set in the past, are happening in the present. Even in trivial matters there are signs of unification that seem novel to outsiders. For example, many Indian languages have the same name for the sun and the moon, and the same word for blue and green.

If we realize that the Potawatomi, for one, actually do distinguish the two colors by saying "green like the grass" and "green like the sky," or that millions of modern Christians find Christ resurrected every Easter, we can put these discoveries in perspective. Nevertheless, popular awareness of them has given tribal thought a reputation for insight and, some feel, a competitive edge over Western philosophies. Such shifts in opinion dovetail with the widely perceived need for a new ethic that can link man with nature, ensuring the conservation of the planet's dwindling resources.

Add to this the ethnic politics of the late twentieth century, and we have a situation where American Indian traditions, at last, need not accommodate to an alien norm. This does not mean that myths are being recited on reservations across the continent and in every city where Indians congregate. Far from it.

Television itself would drown out the traditional stories even if there were no other factors involved, namely the continuing loss of languages and the fragmentation of many communities. But it does mean that traditionalists, who have survived in surprising numbers, are still wanted. And it means that a modern education for Indian children need not exclude myths and ceremonies.

If called upon to explain what must be preserved, Indian people today will often say the fundamental idea is that all things are related. Others, who express themselves in a more traditional manner, will decline to generalize, preferring to make their points by telling stories. In fact there is no other way to keep the tradition genuinely alive. To see it in all its freshness and variety we must go back to the myths themselves.

Notes on Sources

Far from exhaustive, the bibliographies given below include only the principal sources cited in the notes. In an attempt to make them more useful, a dagger (†) has been added to any title that contains an important regional study, and an asterisk (*) denotes an unusually full collection of myths from a particular tribe.

Those who need comprehensive tribal bibliographies may consult Murdock and O'Leary, *Ethnographic Bibliography of North America* (1975). Newer references appear in the *Handbook of North American Indians.* For older lists of works on Indian mythology see Thompson's *The Folktale* and his *Tales of the North American Indians.*

The distribution patterns of major myths, as shown in the maps in this book, may be verified in the notes, keyed to those passages in the text where the myths are discussed. The distributions are not complete in all cases; and if a myth fails to be noted for a tribe or region, this does not necessarily mean it is absent.

A source used in more than one place appears only in the bibliography where it is most applicable. In order to save space, a number of minor sources are not listed in any of the bibliographies and are cited only by one of the following abbreviations (which also help to identify more fully a number of the bibliographic entries):

APAM   Anthropological Papers of the American Museum of Natural History. New York.
ARBAE   Annual Reports of the Bureau of American Ethnology. Washington.
BBAE   Bulletins of the Bureau of American Ethnology. Washington.
CNAI   Curtis, Edward S. *The North American Indian.* 20 vols. Cambridge, Massachusetts (vols. 1–5) and Norwood, Massachusetts (vols. 6–20), 1907–30.
CUCA   Columbia University Contributions to Anthropology. New York.
FMAS   Field (Columbian) Museum (of Natural History) Anthropological Series. Chicago.
HNAI   *Handbook of North American Indians.* Vols. 6 (Subarctic), 1981; 8 (California), 1978; 9 and 10 (Southwest), 1978 and 1983; 15 (Northeast), 1978; remaining volumes forthcoming. Smithsonian Institution, Washington.
JAF   *Journal of American Folklore.*
MAFL   Memoirs of the American Folklore Society. Boston.
PAES   Publications of the American Ethnological Society. New York.
PCES   Papers of the Canadian Ethnology Service. National Museums of Canada, Ottawa.
UCPAAE   University of California Publications in American Archaeology and Ethnology. Berkeley.
YUPA   Yale University Publications in Anthropology. New Haven.

Introduction

Bibliography

Alexander, Hartley Burr. *North American* (vol. 10 of *The Mythology of All Races*, ed. Louis Herbert Gray). Boston: Marshall Jones, 1916.

Boas, Franz. *Race, Language and Culture.* New York: Free Press, 1966. Cited as Boas 1966a.

Hall, Edwin S., Jr.; Margaret B. Blackman; and Vincent Rickard. *Northwest Coast Indian Graphics.* Seattle: University of Washington Press, 1981.

Hultkrantz, Åke. *The North American Indian Orpheus Tradition.* Statens Etnografiska Museum Monograph Series 2. Stockholm. 1957.

Köngäs, Elli K. "The Earth-Diver," *Ethnohistory* 7 (1960): 151–80.

Lévi-Strauss, Claude. *The Raw and the Cooked.* New York: Harper and Row, 1969.

Malinowski, Bronislaw. *Magic, Science and Religion and Other Essays.* Garden City, N.Y.: Doubleday Anchor Books, 1954.

Murdock, George P., and Timothy J. O'Leary. *Ethnographic Bibliography of North America,* 4th ed. 5 vols. New Haven: Human Relations Area Files Press, 1975.

Reichard, Gladys. "Literary Types and the Dissemination of Myths," JAF 34 (1921): 269–307.

Ricketts, Mac Linscott. "The North American Indian Trickster," *History of Religions* 5 (1966): 327–50.

Schmerler, Henrietta. "Trickster Marries His Daughter," JAF 44 (1931): 196–207.

Thompson, Stith. *The Folktale.* New York: Holt, Rinehart and Winston, 1946.

———. *Tales of the North American Indians.* Bloomington: Indiana University Press, 1929.

Utley, Francis Lee. "The Migration of Folktales: Four Channels to the Americas," *Current Anthropology* 15 (1974): 5–27.

Wheelwright, Mary C. *Navajo Creation Myth: The Story of the Emergence by Hasteen Klah.* Santa Fe: Museum of Navajo Cremonial Art, 1942.

Notes

Page 3/"Who would have imagined": quoted in Williams 1956, 308.

Page 3/"Myths have traveled": Boas 1966a, 425.

Page 4/Storytelling performance: see especially Tedlock 1972 (Zuni), Norman 1976 (Cree).

Page 5/Narratives divided into two categories: Rink, 83 (Greenland Eskimo); Hall, 39 (Alaskan Eskimo); Radin 1954, 15 (Winnebago); Dorsey 1906, 13 (Pawnee).

Page 6/Myths regarded as persons: Barbeau 1915, 15–16 (Wyandot); Speck 1935, 34–35 (Penobscot); ARBAE 43 (1928), 189 (Kennebec of Bécancour, Quebec); Gifford 1937, 116 (Coast Yuki); BBAE 171, 384 (Alaskan Eskimo). See also Hallowell, 150 (Ojibwa).

Page 6/Children who fidgeted: de Laguna, 509.

Page 6/Snakes: Adamson, xii (Coast Salish); Barbeau 1915, 5 (Wyandot); Parker 1923, xxvi (Seneca).

Page 7/Old-age deformity: Adamson, xxi (Coast Salish); Tedlock 1972, xvi
   (Zuni); Gifford 1937, 116 (Coast Yuki). See also Barrett, 42 (Pomo).
Page 7/Earth Diver: see Reichard 1921, 274; Thompson 1929, 279; Utley, 8;
   Köngäs; McKennan, 190 (Earth Diver in Alaska). Cf. Spencer 1959, 384
   (North Alaska).
Page 10/Orpheus traced through Asia: see Hultkrantz.
Page 10/Bird Nester: see Lévi-Strauss 1969, Lévi-Strauss 1971.
Page 12/Apache Coyote: MAFL 33, viii.
Page 13/Trickster marries his daughter: see Schmerler.
Page 13/Women of the old school: Lowie 1956, 111.
Page 13/"Has held out with a sense of humor": Jacobs, 129.
Page 13/Omaha Bungling Host: Dorsey 1890, 552-58.
Page 14/Tanana Earth Diver: McKennan, 190.
Page 14/Tight brown leggings: JAF 43 (1930), 429.
Page 15/Wichita creation myth: Dorsey 1904a, 25.
Page 15/Coyote's wife: Lowie 1956, 132.
Page 18/Trickster stands for the shaman: Ricketts, 338.
Page 20/"A warrant, a charter": Malinowski, 108.

Part One: Northwest Coast

Bibliography

[Angus, Charlotte, et al.] *We-gyet Wanders On: Legends of the Northwest.* Seattle:
   Hancock House, 1977.
Barbeau, [Charles] Marius. "Bear Mother," JAF 59 (1945): 1–12.
———. *Totem Poles.* 2 vols. Ottawa: National Museum of Canada, 1950.
Blackman, Margaret B. *Window on the Past: The Photographic Ethnohistory of the
   Northern and Kaigani Haida.* PCES 74. 1981.
Boas, Franz. *Bella Bella Tales.* MAFL 25. 1932.
———. *Kwakiutl Ethnography.* University of Chicago Press, 1966. Cited as Boas
   1966b.
———. *Kwakiutl Tales.* CUCA 2. 1910.
———. *Kwakiutl Tales,* new series. CUCA 26, pt. 1. 1935.
†*———. "Tsimshian Mythology," ARBAE 31 (1916): 29–1037.
de Laguna, Frederica. *Under Mount Saint Elias: The History and Culture of the Yakutat
   Tlingit.* 3 vols. Washington: Smithsonian Institution, 1972.
Halpern, Ida. "Indian Music of the Pacific Northwest Coast." Booklet accompa-
   nying album FE 4523, Folkways Records. New York, 1967.
Hunt, George. "The Rival Chiefs." In *Boas Anniversary Volume,* 108-36. New
   York: G. E. Steckert, 1906.
McClellan, Catharine. *The Girl Who Married a Bear.* Ottawa: National Museums
   of Canada, 1970.
*McIlwraith, T. F. *The Bella Coola Indians.* 2 vols. University of Toronto Press,
   1948.
Rohner, Ronald P., and Evelyn C. Rohner. *The Kwakiutl Indians of British Co-
   lumbia.* New York: Holt, 1970.
Swanton, John R. *Contributions to the Ethnology of the Haida.* Memoirs of the
   American Museum of Natural History 8, pt. 1. 1905.

————. "The Tlingit Indians," ARBAE 26 (1908): 391–485.

*————. *Tlingit Myths and Texts*. BBAE 39. 1909.

[Walkus, Simon, Sr.] *Oowekeeno Oral Traditions: As Told by the Late Chief Simon Walkus Sr.* PCES 84. 1982.

Notes

Page 25/Only the rich told Raven stories: Swanton 1909, 80.

Page 25/Raven thinks of the poor: de Laguna, 842–43.

Page 26/New version of Tsimshian Raven cycle: Angus et al.

Page 26/"Still it's the same": de Laguna, 841.

Page 26/Property Woman: Swanton 1905, 29. Cf. Swanton 1908, 460; Boas 1916, 157.

Page 28/Bird called Property: Swanton 1905, 29.

Page 28/Boas' conjecture: Boas 1966b, 302.

Page 28/Tsimshian Raven cycle: Boas 1916, 58–105. For distribution of Raven myths in other Northwest Coast cultures, see ibid., 567.

Page 32/Haida Raven myth: CNAI 11, 148–49. Cf. Swanton 1905, 73.

Page 34/Raven and Christian influences: McIlwraith 1, 82; Halpern, 15; de Laguna, 842–43.

Page 35/Story of *Kánekelak:* Boas 1935, 1–11, and Boas 1916, 912. Cf. CNAI 10, 247–53. For the Transformer cycle in other Northwest Coast cultures, see Boas 1916, 586–97.

Page 37/Mink story: Boas 1910, 123. For Bella Bella, Bella Coola, Owikeno, and Nootka Mink tales, see Boas 1916, 585.

Page 39/Cry of the *Tsúnukwa:* Boas 1966b, 89.

Page 39/Potlatch oratory: examples are drawn from McIlwraith 1, 167 & 307; Boas 1966b, 81; Hunt, 115–16.

Page 40/Bella Coola ancestor myths: McIlwraith 1, 34–36 & 304.

Page 41/Haida ancestor myths: Swanton 1905, 75 & 94–96; Barbeau 1950 1, 65–68. Cf. Boas 1916, 832–34.

Page 41/Young people in the 1970s: Blackman, 38.

Page 41/Woodworm story: Swanton 1909, 151; de Laguna, 882.

Page 42/Achomawi tale: JAF 44 (1931), 125.

Page 44/Coos story: Frachtenberg 1913, 85.

Page 44/*Tsúnukwa* story: CNAI 10, 296.

Page 45/*Pápakalanósiwa* story: CNAI 10, 165; Walkus, 47.

Page 48/Raven's salmon wife: Boas 1916, 76 & 669.

Page 48/Haida Salmon Boy: Swanton 1905, 243. For distribution, see Boas 1916, 770.

Page 49/"Fish Commissioner thinks he knows": de Laguna, 890.

Page 50/Story of *Kats:* Swanton 1909, 228.

Page 50/Tlingit Bear Mother myth: de Laguna, 880 & 882. For distribution, see McClellan, 58.

Page 53/"Exuberant" diversity: Boas 1932, viii. Cf. Boas 1940, 423n.

Page 53/"Mythological worlds": Boas 1940, 424.

Part Two: Far North

Eskimo Bibliography

Boas, Franz. *The Central Eskimo.* Lincoln: University of Nebraska Press, 1964.
†————. *The Eskimo of Baffin Land and Hudson Bay.* Bulletin of the American Museum of Natural History 15, pts. 1 & 2. 1901–7.
Golder, F. A. "Aleutian Stories," JAF 18 (1905): 215–22.
Hall, Edwin S., Jr. *The Eskimo Storyteller: Folktales from Noatak, Alaska.* Knoxville: University of Tennessee Press, 1975.
Jenness, D. "Myths and Traditions from Northern Alaska, the Mackenzie Delta and Coronation Gulf." Report of the Canadian Arctic Expedition 1913–18, vol. 13 *(Eskimo Folklore),* pt. A. 1924.
†Lantis, Margaret. "The Mythology of Kodiak Island, Alaska," JAF 51 (1938): 123–72.
————. *The Social Culture of the Nunivak Eskimo.* Transactions of the American Philosophical Society, n.s., vol. 35, pt. 3. 1946.
Lutz, Maija M. *The Effects of Acculturation on Eskimo Music of Cumberland Peninsula.* PCES 41. 1978.
Murdoch, John. "A Few Legendary Fragments from Point Barrow Eskimos," *American Naturalist* 20 (1886): 593–99.
Nelson, Edward W. "The Eskimo About Bering Strait," ARBAE 18 (1899): 3–518.
Rasmussen, Knud. *Eskimo Folk-Tales* (W. Worster, trans.). London and Copenhagen: Gyldendal, 1921.
————. *Intellectual Culture of the Caribou Eskimos.* Copenhagen: Gyldendal, 1930.
————. *Observations on the Intellectual Culture of the Copper Eskimos.* Copenhagen: Gyldendal, 1932.
————. *Intellectual Culture of the Iglulik Eskimos.* Copenhagen: Gyldendal, 1929.
————. *The Netsilik Eskimos.* Copenhagen: Gyldendal, 1931.
Rink, Henry. *Tales and Traditions of the Eskimo.* Edinburgh and London: Blackwood, 1875.
Spalding, Alex. *Eight Inuit Myths.* PCES 59. 1979.
Spencer, Robert F. *The North Alaskan Eskimo.* BBAE 171. 1959.
Turner, Lucien M. "Ethnology of the Ungava District, Hudson Bay Territory," ARBAE 11 (1894): 159–350.

Athapascan Bibliography

Boas, Franz. "Traditions of the Ts'ets'aut," JAF 9 (1896): 257–68.
Cruikshank, Julie. *The Stolen Women: Female Journeys in Tagish and Tutchone.* PCES 87. 1983.
Jenness, D. "Myths of the Carrier Indians of British Columbia," JAF 47 (1934): 97–257.
Jetté, Jules. "On Ten'a Folklore," *Journal of the Royal Anthropological Institute of Great Britain and Ireland,* n.s., vol. 38 (1908): 298–320.
McKennan, Robert A. *The Upper Tanana Indians.* YUPA 55. 1959.
Osgood, Cornelius. *The Han Indians.* YUPA 74. 1971.

*Petitot, Émile. *Traditions indiennes du Canada Nord-Ouest.* Paris: Maisonneuve Frères & Ch. LeClerc, 1886.

Ridington, Robin. *Swan People: A Study of the Dunne-za Prophet Dance.* PCES 38. 1978.

Teit, James. "Kaska Tales," JAF 30 (1917): 427–73.

———. "Tahltan Tales," JAF 32 (1919): 198–250; 34 (1921): 223–53, 335–56.

Williamson, Robert G. "Slave Indian Legends," *Anthropologica* 1 (1955): 119–43.

Notes

Page 58/Storytelling as a soporific: Rasmussen 1931, 363; 1929, 251; 1921, 6.

Page 58/Koyukon storytelling: Jetté, 298–300 & 305.

Page 58/"The earth was as it is": Rasmussen 1931, 209.

Page 60/Origin of Daylight: ibid., 208. Cf. Rasmussen 1929, 253; Jenness 1934, 78.

Page 60/Male progenitors: Rasmussen 1929, 252.

Page 60/Thunder Girls: Rasmussen 1921, 111. Cf. Lantis 1938, 135; Lantis 1946, 269; Murdoch, 595; Rasmussen 1930, 80; Rasmussen 1931, 377; Boas 1964, 192.

Page 60/Sun Sister and Moon Brother: Boas 1964, 189. Cf. Lantis 1938, 136; Lantis 1946, 268; Rasmussen 1930, 79; Rasmussen 1929, 77; Rasmussen 1931, 232; Spalding, 48; Golder, 222. For further distribution, see Boas 1901–7, 359.

Page 60/Origin of Nunivak: CNAI 20, 74. Cf. ibid., 77; Lantis 1946, 265 & 314.

Page 61/*Sila:* Rasmussen 1931, 224, 1929, 62.

Page 61/Raven spears earth: Spencer 1959, 384. Cf. CNAI 20, 214.

Page 61/Man emerges from pod: Nelson, 452.

Page 61/Origin of Kodiak Island: Lantis 1938, 131.

Page 63/Egg Woman: Petitot, 109.

Page 63/Mcat Mother: Teit 1919, 230. Cf. HNAI 6, 479.

Page 64/*Sedna* myth: Boas 1964, 175 & 229. Cf. Turner, 261; Rink, 39–40; Rasmussen 1921, 113; Rasmussen 1929, 63; Rasmussen 1931, 225 & 227; Rasmussen 1932, 24–27 (ritual only, no myth). For further distribution, see Thompson 1929, 272–73 (Thompson erroneously includes Alaska).

Page 64/Baffin Island Eskimo today: Lutz, 97–116.

Page 66/Tagish variant: Cruikshank, 28. Cf. Boas 1896, 260; Osgood, 117; Williamson, 123.

Page 68/Humans from punctured fish: Petitot, 150. Cf. ibid., 36.

Page 68/Raven hoards game: Teit 1917, 441. Cf. Petitot, 154 & 379.

Page 68/Arrow cycle: Osgood, 117; Williamson, 132; Petitot, 321. Cf. Petitot, 141.

Page 68/Kaska version: Teit 1917, 440–41.

Page 68/Temptress has mink and weasel: Teit 1917, 435.

Page 69/Two Brothers tale of the Chipewyan: Petitot, 352.

Page 69/Transformer cycle of the Beaver Indians: Ridington, 17 & 58 & 116–19.

Page 71/Ahtna copper legend: de Laguna, 889. See also ibid., 230–31.

Page 71/Copper Woman: CNAI 18, 127. Cf. Petitot, 412 & 417; HNAI 6, 302.

Page 71/Dog Husband: Petitot, 311. For further Athapascan distribution, see

Jenness 1934, 137; McKennan, 162; HNAI 6, 279. For Northwest Coast, Plateau, and Plains distribution, see Boas 1916, 586 (Chilcotin); de Laguna, 875 (Tlingit); Reichard 1947, 126; Thompson 1929, 347.

Part Three: Southwest

Bibliography

Bahr, Donald M. *Pima and Papago Ritual Oratory.* San Francisco: Indian Historian Press, 1975.
Benedict, Ruth. *Patterns of Culture.* New York: New American Library, 1960.
*———. *Zuni Mythology.* 2 vols. CUCA 21. 1935.
Blackburn, Thomas C., ed. *December's Child: A Book of Chumash Oral Narratives.* Berkeley: University of California Press, 1975.
Courlander, Harold. *Hopi Voices.* Albuquerque: University of New Mexico Press, 1982.
Densmore, Frances. *Papago Music.* BBAE 90. 1929.
Farrer, Claire R. "Singing for Life." In Charlotte J. Frisbie, ed., *Southwestern Indian Ritual Drama.* Albuquerque: University of New Mexico Press, 1980.
Gifford, Edward W. *The Southeastern Yavapai.* UCPAAE 29. 1932.
Goddard, P. E. *Myths and Tales from the White Mountain Apache.* APAM 24, pt. 2. 1919.
———. *Navajo Texts.* APAM 34, pt. 1. 1933.
Johnston, Bernice E. *California's Gabrielino Indians.* Los Angeles: Southwest Museum, 1962.
*Matthews, Washington. *Navaho Legends.* MAFL 5. 1897.
*Opler, Morris E. *Myths and Tales of the Jicarilla Apache Indians.* MAFL 31. 1938.
Parsons, Elsie C. *Taos Tales.* MAFL 34. 1940.
———. *Tewa Tales.* MAFL 19. 1926.
Reichard, Gladys A. *Navajo Medicine Man Sandpaintings.* New York: Dover, 1977.
Spencer, Katherine. *Mythology and Values: An Analysis of Navaho Chantway Myths.* MAFL 48. 1957.
Stirling, Matthew W. *Origin Myth of Acoma and Other Records.* BBAE 135. 1942.
Tedlock, Dennis. *Finding the Center: Narrative Poetry of the Zuni Indians.* New York: Dial, 1972.
———. *The Spoken Word and the Work of Interpretation.* Philadelphia: University of Pennsylvania Press, 1983.
Underhill, Ruth M. *Papago Indian Religion.* New York: Columbia University Press, 1946.
———. *Red Man's Religion.* Chicago: University of Chicago Press. 1965.
*Voth, H. R. *The Traditions of the Hopi.* FMAS 8. 1905.
Wyman, Leland C. *Blessingway.* Tucson: University of Arizona Press, 1970.
Yazzie, Ethelou, ed. *Navajo History,* vol. 1. Written under the direction of the Navajo Curriculum Center, Rough Rock Demonstration School. Many Farms, Arizona: Navajo Community College Press, 1971.
Zuni People. *The Zunis: Self-Portrayals.* Albuquerque: University of New Mexico Press, 1970.

Notes

Page 80/Composite version of Navajo Emergence: Yazzie. For bibliographical note on 28 other Navajo versions, see HNAI 10, 505.

Page 80/Hopi Emergence: Voth, 10 & 16.

Page 82/Zuni *Kyáklo* ritual: ARBAE 23 (1905), 65–78; Tedlock 1983, 235.

Page 82/Jicarilla Emergence: Opler, 1–27. For Lipan version, see MAFL 36 (1940). For Yavapai, see Gifford 1932, 243; HNAI 10, 51.

Page 82/Keresan and Isleta versions: Stirling; ARBAE 11 (1894), 26 (Zia); BBAE 98, 1 & 203 (Cochiti); JAF 41 (1928), 288 (San Felipe); HNAI 9, 404 (Santa Ana); HNAI 9, 383 (Santo Domingo); ARBAE 47 (1932), 359 (Isleta).

Page 82/"This corn is my heart": ARBAE 11 (1894), 39.

Page 83/Navajo *yéi* create humans: Matthews, 69.

Page 84/Jicarilla creation: Opler, 1.

Page 84/*Awonawilona:* ARBAE 13 (1896), 379. See also ARBAE 23 (1905), 23. Cf. ARBAE 47 (1932), 486n; HNAI 9, 499 (for singular and plural forms).

Page 85/Mescalero population: Farrer, 125–26.

Page 86/Western Apache Bird Nester myth: Goddard 1919, 132. Cf. Spencer, 194.

Page 91/"It was named water": Goddard 1933, 127.

Page 91/"They came to the [lowest] world": Benedict 1935 1, 2.

Page 92/Ruth Benedict: Benedict 1960, 80 & 86.

Page 92/Gladys Reichard: JAF 56 (1943), 17.

Page 94/Chumash monster-ridding cycle: Blackburn, 104–155.

Page 95/Papago Flute Lure: Densmore 1929, 54. For variants, see Gayton 1935a, 587 (Serrano, Diegueño, Havasupai, Yavapai, Maricopa, Shivwits, Southern Ute); see also JAF 49 (1936), 331 (Pima).

Page 96/Rare Hopi version: JAF 42(1929), 3.

Page 96/Pokangs scare grandmother: Courlander, 216.

Page 97/Storytelling in Taos: Parsons 1940, 1.

Page 98/Changing Woman and the twins: this composite summary of the Navajo monster-ridding cycle is drawn mainly from Yazzie; Matthews; Wyman; and CNAI 1, 98. For variant monster-ridding cycles of the Navajo type, see Opler, 44 (Jicarilla); MAFL 36 (1940), 13 (Lipan); HNAI 10, 433 (Mescalero); HNAI 10, 416 (Chiricahua); Goddard 1918, 36 (Western Apache); Goddard 1919, 115 (Western Apache); Benedict 1935 1, 285 (Zuni); ARBAE 11 (1894), 43–53 (Zia); BBAE 98, 211 (Cochiti).

Page 101/Zuni emergence and first death: ARBAE 13 (1896), 383; Benedict 1935 1, 258.

Page 101/Gabrielino and Luiseño Dying God: Johnston, 40; JAF 18 (1905), 312; JAF 19 (1906), 59; CNAI 15, 20.

Page 101/Cutting a piece from the corpse: Kroeber 1925, 643.

Page 102/Mojave Dying God: ibid., 770. See also CNAI 2, 53; JAF 18 (1905), 314; HNAI 10, 65. For other Yuman versions, see CNAI 15, 51 & 121 (Diegueño); CNAI 2, 73 (Yuma), 86 (Maricopa), 102 (Havasupai); Gifford 1932, 245 (Yavapai); HNAI 10, 25–26 (Walapai).

Page 103/Modern Mojave cremation: Underhill 1965, 67; HNAI 10, 68.
Page 103/Dying God of the inland Takic: CNAI 15, 36 & 105 (Cahuilla); Kroeber 1925, 619 (Serrano), 692 (Cupeño).
Page 103/Piman creation story: Underhill 1946, 8 & 135; Bahr, 31; ARBAE 26 (1908), 206; Densmore 1929, 17.
Page 104/Piman theory of disease: Bahr, 4; HNAI 10, 199.
Page 105/Cahuilla creation: CNAI 15, 106.
Page 105/Piman creation: ARBAE 26 (1908), 206.
Page 105/Luiseño creation: Kroeber 1925, 677: JAF 19 (1906), 52.
Page 106/Montezuma: HNAI 9, 619.
Page 106/Tewa story: Parsons 1926, 108.
Page 106/Montezuma as dying god: JAF 34 (1921), 255; Underhill 1946, 12.
Page 106/*Póshayanki:* ARBAE 13 (1896), 381.

Part Four: West Central

Bibliography

Angulo, Jaime de. "Indians in Overalls," *Hudson Review* 3 (1950): 327–79.
———. "Pomo Creation Myth," JAF 48 (1935): 203–62.
†*Barrett, S. A. *Pomo Myths.* Bulletin of the Public Museum of the City of Milwaukee 15. 1933.
Curtin, Jeremiah. *Creation Myths of Primitive America.* Boston: Little, Brown, 1903.
Dangberg, Grace. "Washo Texts." UCPAAE 22:391–443. 1927.
Demetracopoulou, D. "The Loon Woman Myth," JAF 46 (1933): 101–28.
Du Bois, Cora. "Wintu Ethnography." UCPAAE 36: 1–148. 1935.
———, and D. Demetracopoulou. "Wintu Myths." UCPAAE 28: 279–403. 1931.
†Gayton, A. H. "Areal Affiliations of California Folktales," *American Anthropologist,* n.s., 37 (1935): 582–99. Cited as Gayton 1935a.
Gifford, E. W. "Coast Yuki Myths," JAF 50 (1937): 115–72.
———. "Miwok Myths." UCPAAE 12: 283–338. 1917.
———. "Western Mono Myths," JAF 36 (1923): 301–67.
Goddard, P. E. "Kato Texts." UCPAAE 5: 65–238. 1909.
†Heizer, Robert F. "[California] Mythology." HNAI 8: 654–57. 1978.
Kardiner, Abram, and Edward Preble. *They Studied Man.* Cleveland: World, 1961.
Kroeber, A. L. *Handbook of the Indians of California.* BBAE 78. 1925.
†———. "Indian Myths of South Central California." UCPAAE 4: 167–250. 1907.
Loeb, Edwin M. "The Eastern Kuksu Cult." UCPAAE 33: 139–232. 1933.
Lowie, Robert H. "The Northern Shoshone." APAM 2: 169–306. 1908.
*———. "Shoshonean Tales," JAF 37 (1924): 1–242.
Mason, J. Alden. "The Ethnology of the Salinan Indians." UCPAAE 10: 97–240. 1912.
Merriam, C. Hart. *An-nik-a-del.* Boston: Stratford, 1928.

Radin, Paul. "Wappo Texts." UCPAAE 19: 1–147. 1924.
Steward, Julian H. "Myths of the Owens Valley Paiute." UCPAAE 34: 355–440. 1936.
———. "Some Western Shoshoni Myths." BBAE 136: 249–99. 1943.
Voegelin, Charles F. "Tübatulabal Texts." UCPAAE 34: 191–246. 1935.

Notes

Page 114/"He walked over the hill": Angulo 1935, 237.
Page 114/"Then the old man": Merriam, 114.
Page 116/Coast Miwok story: HNAI 8, 422.
Page 116/Wappo myth: Radin 1924, 45.
Page 116/Earth Diver: Gayton 1935a, 588 (Tubatulabal, Mono, Salinan, Yokuts, Miwok, Patwin, Maidu, Wintu); Barrett 1933, 467 (Pomo); Clark 1966, 172 (Eastern Shoshone).
Page 116/Humans from sticks: Radin 1924, 45. For further distribution, see Gayton 1935a, 590–91; Barrett 1933, 469.
Page 116/Lizard hand: Kroeber 1907, 231. For further distribution, see Barrett 1933, 470; Gayton 1935a, 589.
Page 116/Origin of death: Steward 1936, 368. For further distribution, see JAF 30 (1917), 486–91.
Page 116/Salinan epic: Mason, 192.
Page 117/"Prairie Falcon told his people": Gifford 1917, 310.
Page 117/Mallard girls: Barrett 1933, 43.
Page 118/"She saw a hair": Demetracopoulou, 104; for distribution of Loon Woman, see ibid., 102–3.
Page 120/"Crazy woman, Loon": Angulo 1950, 371.
Page 120/Norelputus: Du Bois, 72 & 79; Du Bois & Demetracopoulou, 281. The myths of Norelputus are in Curtin.
Page 120/World's Heart: Merriam, 114.
Page 120/*Madúmda:* Barrett 1933, 18.
Page 120/*Taikómol:* CNAI 14, 169. For "Taikómol school," see Kroeber 1925, 184.
Page 121/*Nágaicho:* Goddard 1909, 183.
Page 121/Maidu creation story: JAF 16 (1903), 32–33; Loeb, 197; Kroeber 1925, 183.
Page 121/"What is this thing . . . ?": Angulo 1950, 369.
Page 123/Cottontail story: CNAI 15, 143. See also Steward 1936, 371 (Mono); Clark 1966, 179 (Eastern Shoshone); Lowie 1924, 142 (Shivwits).
Page 124/*Hainanu* et al.: Gifford 1923, 303–4; Lowie 1908; Steward 1936, 361; CNAI 15, 135.
Page 124/Death of Wolf: CNAI 15, 148; Steward 1943, 297; Lowie 1924, 92 (Shivwits). For further distribution, see Gayton 1935a, 594.
Page 125/Myth of the island woman: Lowie 1924, 157 (Moapa); see also Gayton 1935a, 593 (Chemehuevi, Mono, Kaibab, Shivwits, Paviotso, Washo, Southern Ute, Northern Shoshone); Steward 1943, 262 (Panamint) & 267 (Gosiute).
Page 126/People Mother: CNAI 15, 129 (Paviotso). For further distribution, see

Gayton 1935a, 593 (Tubatulabal, Mono, Paviotso); UCPAAE 36, 335 (Washo); Dangberg, 395 (Washo).
Page 127/Steward's essay: Steward 1936, 356–63.
Page 127/"Then I went to the Bella Coolas": quoted in Kardiner and Preble, 148.

Part Five: Coast-Plateau

Bibliography

Adamson, Thelma. *Folk-Tales of the Coast Salish.* MAFL 27. 1934.

Armellada, Cesáreo de. *Pemontón taremarú: Invocaciones mágicos de los indios pemón.* Caracas: Universidad Católica Andrés Bello, 1972.

Ballard, Arthur C. "Mythology of Southern Puget Sound." University of Washington Publications in Anthropology 3: 31–150. Seattle, 1929.

Boas, Franz. *Chinook Texts.* BBAE 20. 1894.

———. *Folk-Tales of Salishan and Sahaptin Tribes.* MAFL 11. 1917.

———. *Kathlamet Texts.* BBAE 26. 1901.

———. *Kutenai Tales.* BBAE 59. 1918.

Clark, Ella E. *Indian Legends from the Northern Rockies.* Norman: University of Oklahoma Press, 1966.

———. *Indian Legends of the Pacific Northwest.* Berkeley: University of California Press, 1953.

Drucker, Philip. "The Tolowa and Their Southwest Oregon Kin." UCPAAE 36: 221–300. 1937.

Frachtenberg, Leo J. *Coos Texts.* CUCA 1. 1913.

———. "Kalapuya Texts." University of Washington Publications in Anthropology 11: 143–369. Seattle, 1945.

Gayton, A. H. "The Orpheus Myth in North America," JAF 48 (1935): 263–93. Cited as Gayton 1935b.

Goddard, P. E. "Hupa Texts." UCPAAE 1: 89–368. 1904.

*Jacobs, Melville. *Coos Myth Texts.* University of Washington Publications in Anthropology 8: 127–260. Seattle, 1940.

*Kroeber, A. L. *Yurok Myths.* Berkeley: University of California Press, 1976.

*———, and E. W. Gifford. *Karok Myths.* Berkeley: University of California Press, 1980.

†Lévi-Strauss, Claude. *L'Homme nu* (Mythologiques 4). Paris: Plon, 1971.

Ray, Verne F. "Sanpoil Folk Tales," JAF 46 (1933): 129–87.

†Reichard, Gladys. *An Analysis of Coeur d'Alene Indian Myths.* MAFL 41. 1947.

Spier, Leslie. *The Prophet Dance of the Northwest and Its Derivatives.* Menasha, Wisc.: George Banta, 1935.

Teit, James. "Mythology of the Thompson Indians." Memoirs of the American Museum of Natural History 12: 199–416. 1912.

———. "The Shuswap." Memoirs of the American Museum of Natural History 4: 447–758. 1909.

———. *Traditions of the Thompson River Indians of British Columbia.* MAFL 6. 1898.

Turney-High, Harry. "The Bluejay Dance," *American Anthropologist,* n.s. 35 (1933): 103–7.

Notes

Page 134/"Coyote continued his travels": CNAI 8, 116.

Page 136/"Beautify" the earth: CNAI 9, 119 & 120.

Page 136/The Moon epic: Ballard, 69. For variants, see CNAI 9, 117; Adamson, 158.

Page 137/Salish root child: Reichard 1947, 57–65.

Page 138/Tolowa root child: Drucker, 268.

Page 138/Dug-from-Ground: see Thompson 1929, 314.

Page 138/Story of *Musp* and *Komól:* CNAI 8, 116; Boas 1894, 17. For Salish variants, see Adamson, 329; Boas 1916, 587.

Page 140/Stories of Jesus the traveler: Adamson, 138–39.

Page 142/Bluejay Dance: Turney-High. See also Clark 1966, 96.

Page 142/Myth of the Hupa culture hero: Goddard 1904, 123.

Page 143/Sanpoil salmon release: Boas 1917, 101. For variants, see ibid., 67 (Okanagon) & 139 (Nez Percé); Boas 1918, 172 (Kutenai); CNAI 14, 167 (Wailaki).

Page 144/Chinook Orpheus myth: CNAI 8, 126. For variants, see Gayton 1935b (Puyallup, Thompson, Okanagon, Tillamook, Alsea, Coos, Karok, Hupa, Shasta, Klamath, Klikitat, etc.); Frachtenberg 1945, 199 (Kalapuya).

Page 145/Bird Nester: Boas 1917, 120 (Coeur d'Alene) & 135 (Nez Percé); Teit 1898, 21 (Thompson); Teit 1909, 622 & 737 (Shuswap); Jacobs, 245–46 (Coos); Kroeber and Gifford, 339 (Karok, Yurok); Lévi-Strauss 1971, 623–34 (Klamath, Cowlitz, Alsea, etc.); JAF 32 (1919), 348 (Wailaki).

Page 145/Yurok Bird Nester with money theme: Kroeber 1976, 287–89; Kroeber 1925, 73.

Page 145/Woman Who Washed Her Face: Adamson, 2. Cf. ibid., 1 & 178; Ballard 49–50.

Page 146/Chinook myth of Panther and Beaver: Boas 1901, 20. Cf. CNAI 9, 125.

Page 146/Klamath story of Gopher: CNAI 13, 210.

Page 146/Okanagon myth of Old One: Boas 1917, 80. For similar Salish and Sahaptian myths of world creation, see Teit 1912, 322 (Thompson); Boas 1917, 120 (Coeur d'Alene); Ray, 132 (Sanpoil); Clark 1966, 37 (Nez Percé) & 66 (Flathead); Clark 1953, 143 (Yakima).

Page 146/Chastacosta creation myth: JAF 28 (1915), 224. Cf. Drucker, 268 (Tolowa); Frachtenberg 1913, 5 (Coos).

Page 147/Five world ages: Jacobs, 173 (Coos); Frachtenberg 1945, 173 (Kalapuya); CNAI 14, 169 (Yuki); Angulo 1935 (Pomo); Du Bois 1935, 74 (Wintu); Clark 1966, 66 (Flathead).

Page 148/Karok myth-formula: Kroeber and Gifford, 270. On tale-type formulas, see also Kroeber 1925, 4 & 72 (Yurok); Kroeber 1976, 488 (Yurok); HNAI 8, 220 (Shasta); Armellada (Arekuna).

Part Six: Plains

Bibliography

Bowers, Alfred W. *Mandan Social and Ceremonial Organization.* Chicago: University of Chicago Press, 1950.

Brown, Joseph Epes. *The Sacred Pipe: Black Elk's Account of the Seven Rites of the Oglala Sioux.* Norman: University of Oklahoma Press, 1953.

Catlin, George. *Letters and Notes on the Manners, Customs, and Conditions of the North American Indians.* 2 vols. New York: Dover, 1973.

———. *O-kee-pa: A Religious Ceremony and Other Customs of the Mandan.* Lincoln: University of Nebraska Press, 1976.

Dorsey, George A. *The Cheyenne,* pt. 1: Ceremonial Organization. FMAS 9, no. 1. 1905. Cited as Dorsey 1905a.

*———. *The Mythology of the Wichita.* Washington: Carnegie Institution of Washington, 1904. Cited as Dorsey 1904a.

*———. *The Pawnee: Mythology.* Washington: Carnegie Institution of Washington, 1906.

*———. *Traditions of the Arikara.* Washington: Carnegie Institution of Washington, 1904. Cited as Dorsey 1904b.

———. *Traditions of the Caddo.* Washington: Carnegie Institution of Washington, 1905. Cited as Dorsey 1905b.

*———. *Traditions of the Skidi Pawnee.* MAFL 7. 1904. Cited as Dorsey 1904c.

*———, and Alfred L. Kroeber. *Traditions of the Arapaho.* FMAS 5. 1903.

Gilmore, Melvin R. "The Arikara Book of Genesis." Papers of the Michigan Academy of Sciences, Arts, and Letters 12: 95–120. 1929.

Grinnell, George Bird. *Blackfoot Lodge Tales.* Lincoln: University of Nebraska Press, 1962.

———. *By Cheyenne Campfires.* Lincoln: University of Nebraska Press, 1971.

———. *The Cheyenne Indians.* 2 vols. Lincoln: University of Nebraska Press, 1972.

Lame Deer, John (Fire), and Richard Erdoes. *Lame Deer: Seeker of Visions.* New York: Simon and Schuster, 1972.

Linton Ralph. *The Thunder Ceremony of the Pawnee.* Anthropology Leaflet 5. Chicago: Field Museum of Natural History, 1922.

Lowie, Robert H. *The Crow Indians.* New York: Holt, Rinehart and Winston, 1956.

McClintock, Walter. *The Old North Trail.* Lincoln: University of Nebraska Press, 1968.

Momaday, N. Scott. *The Way to Rainy Mountain.* New York: Ballantine Books, 1970.

Mooney, James. *The Ghost-Dance Religion and the Sioux Outbreak of 1890* (Anthony F. C. Wallace, ed.). Chicago: University of Chicago Press, 1965.

Murie, James R. *Ceremonies of the Pawnee* (Douglas R. Parks, ed.). 2 vols. Washington: Smithsonian Institution, 1981.

Riggs, Stephen Return. *Dakota Grammar, Texts, and Ethnography.* Contributions to North American Ethnology 9. Washington, 1893.

Simms, S. C. *Traditions of the Crows.* FMAS 2, no. 6. 1903.

Smith, J. L. "A Short History of the Sacred Calf Pipe of the Teton Dakota," *Museum News* 28 (1967), nos. 7–8. Vermillion, S.D.: W. H. Over Dakota Museum, University of South Dakota.

Steinmetz, Paul B. *Pipe, Bible, and Peyote Among the Oglala Lakota.* Stockholm Studies in Comparative Religion 19. University of Stockholm, 1980.

Thompson, Stith. "The Star Husband Tale." In Alan Dundes, ed., *The Study of Folklore.* Englewood Cliffs, N.J.: Prentice-Hall, 1965.

Walker, James R. *Lakota Belief and Ritual* (Raymond J. DeMallie and Elaine A. Jahner, eds.). Lincoln: University of Nebraska Press, 1980.

————. *Lakota Myth* (Elaine A. Jahner, ed.). Lincoln: University of Nebraska Press, 1983.

Weltfish, Gene. *The Lost Universe: The Way of Life of the Pawnee.* New York: Ballantine Books, 1971.

Wheeler-Voegelin, Ermine, and Remedios W. Moore. "The Emergence Myth in Native North America." In W. Edson Richmond, ed., *Studies in Folklore.* Bloomington: Indiana University Press, 1957.

Wissler, Clark. *Star Legends Among the American Indians.* Guide Leaflet 91. New York: American Museum of Natural History, 1936.

Notes

Page 153/Wichita storytelling session: Dorsey 1904a, 23.

Page 154/Spider: FMAS 4 (Arapaho); CNAI 5, 134 (Gros Ventre); APAM 1, pt. 3 (Gros Ventre); Walker 1980, 123–24 (Lakota Sioux) & 296 (Yankton Sioux, Santee Sioux); APAM 4, pt. 1 (Assiniboin); Grinnell 1971, 281 (Cheyenne).

Page 154/Earth Diver: for Plains distribution, see Thompson 1929, 279 (Arapaho, Hidatsa, Blackfeet, Sarcee, Gros Ventre, Assiniboin, Crow, Arikara, Cheyenne); Bowers, 347 (Mandan).

Page 154/Women's Camp: Grinnell 1971, 284.

Page 154/Mourner's Haircut: CNAI 5, 138–39 (Gros Ventre).

Page 154/Mice's Sun Dance: Dorsey and Kroeber, 107.

Page 154/Fat, Grease, and Berries: Simms, 285.

Page 156/*Kawaharu* tales: Dorsey 1906, 141; see also Murie, 71.

Page 156/"There was a poor, lame, one-eyed boy": Dorsey 1904c, 65.

Page 156/Half-a-Boy: Dorsey 1904a, 194.

Page 157/Lodge Boy and Thrown Away: Wissler, 20 (Blackfeet); Simms, 303 (Crow); Dorsey 1904a, 33 (Wichita); CNAI 18, 136 (Sarcee); FMAS 1, 77 (Gros Ventre); Dorsey and Kroeber, 341 (Arapaho); PAES 9, 134 (Lakota Sioux); Reichard 1921, 273 (Hidatsa, Assiniboin, Pawnee).

Page 157/Northwestern California myth: UCPAAE 1, 126 (Hupa); Kroeber and Gifford, 339 (Karok, Yurok).

Page 159/Star Boy (Moon Boy, Sun Boy): Thompson 1965, 426–32 (Assiniboin, Arikara, Hidatsa, Cheyenne, Santee Sioux, Pawnee); Simms, 299 (Crow); FMAS 1, 94 (Gros Ventre); FMAS 4, 212 (Arapaho); Bowers, 200 (Mandan). For Blackfeet Scarface, see McClintock, 491; Grinnell 1962, 93. For Kiowa Split Boys, see MAFL 22, 1; Momaday, 26–45.

Page 160/"My grandfather, Light of the World": FMAS 4, 36.

Page 161/Arapaho and Cheyenne Sun Dance: FMAS 4, 191–212 (Arapaho); Grinnell 1972 2, 258 (Cheyenne).

Page 164/Lone Man: Bowers, 347–53; see also CNAI 5, 48.

Page 164/"I might write much more": Catlin 1973 1, 182.

Page 165/Heavy woman: BBAE 194, 298–312 (Hidatsa); MAFL 32, 18 (Hidatsa); Catlin 1973 1, 179 (Mandan); BBAE 30, pt. 1, 797 (Mandan); JAF 90 (1977), 162–63 (Lakota Sioux); Grinnell 1971, 242 (Cheyenne); ARBAE 17 (1898), 152–53 (Kiowa).

Page 166/"Yes, I thought, now I see the earth": Momaday, 19.

Page 166/Arikara emergence story: Gilmore; Dorsey 1904b, 12. For Pawnee and Wichita emergence stories, see Wheeler-Voegelin and Moore, 84. For Caddo, see Dorsey 1905b, 8.

Page 167/"Reverence and gratitude": Gilmore, 99.

Page 167/"Mother has undone her belt": CNAI 5, 71.

Page 167/Skidi creation ceremony: Murie 1, 43–62; Linton.

Page 167/Myth of Tiráwahat: Dorsey 1904c, 3; see also Murie 1, 179 n. 16.

Page 169/Murie: Murie 1, 21; Weltfish, 584.

Page 169/"Ancient Egypt, Greece, and Rome": Walker 1980, 292.

Page 169/Walker's cosmogony: Walker 1980, 39 & 50–54 & 115; JAF 90 (1977): 149–67; Walker 1983, 191–383.

Page 170/Story of Wi: APAM 16, 164; Lame Deer and Erdoes, 30.

Page 172/Prophecies: Mooney (Ghost Dance); Spier, 9 (Coast-Plateau); Ridington (Beaver); Dorsey 1906 (Pawnee); Brown, 9 (Lakota Sioux); Dorsey 1904a, 21–22 & 26–27 (Wichita).

Page 174/Arapaho Flat Pipe: Mooney, 207; FMAS 4, 191; Dorsey and Kroeber, 1.

Page 174/Buffalo Cap: Dorsey 1905a, 46.

Page 178/Sacred Arrows: JAF 21 (1908), 271.

Page 178/Buffalo Wife: Grinnell 1971, 87. For distribution, see Thompson 1929, 339 n. 222.

Page 178/Calf Pipe: CNAI 3, 56 (Elk Head's version of the legend); cf. Brown, 3. For the similar Wichita myth, see CNAI 19, 93. For the Calf Pipe in recent years, see Smith; Steinmetz, 17–18.

Part Seven: East

Bibliography

*Barbeau, Charles Marius. *Huron and Wyandot Mythology.* Canada, Department of Mines, Geological Survey, Memoir 80; Anthropological Series 11. 1915.

Brinton, Daniel G. *The Lenâpé and Their Legends.* Philadelphia: D. G. Brinton, 1884.

Bushnell, David I. "Myths of the Louisiana Choctaw," *American Anthropologist,* n.s. 12 (1910): 526–35.

†Fisher, Margaret W. "The Mythology of the Northern and Northeastern Algonkians . . ." In Frederick Johnson, ed., *Man in Northeastern North America,* Papers of the Robert S. Peabody Foundation for Archaeology 3: 226–62. Andover, Mass., 1946.

Flannery, Regina. *An Analysis of Coastal Algonquian Culture.* Catholic University of America, Anthropological Series 7. 1939.

Haas, Mary R. "The Solar Deity of the Tunica." Papers of the Michigan Academy of Sciences, Arts, and Letters 28: 531–35. 1942.

Halbert, H. S. "The Choctaw Creation Legend." Publications of the Mississippi Historical Society 4: 267–70. Oxford, Miss. 1901.

Haviland, William A., and Marjory W. Power. *The Original Vermonters.* University Press of New England, 1981.

Hewitt, J. N. B. "Iroquoian Cosmology," pt. 1, ARBAE 21 (1903): 127–339.

———. "Iroquoian Cosmology," pt. 2, ARBAE 43 (1928): 449–819.

*———, ed. "Seneca Fiction, Legends, and Myths," ARBAE 32 (1918): 37–813.

Kilpatrick, Jack F., and Anna G. Kilpatrick. *Friends of Thunder: Folktales of the Oklahoma Cherokees.* Dallas: Southern Methodist University Press, 1964.

Kinietz, Vernon, and Erminie W. Voegelin. *Shawnese Traditions: C. C. Trowbridge's Account.* Occasional Contributions from the Museum of Anthropology of the University of Michigan 9. 1939.

Leland, Charles G. *The Algonquin Legends of New England.* Boston: Houghton Mifflin, 1884.

Mechling, W. H. *Malecite Tales.* Canada, Department of Mines, Geological Survey, Memoir 49, Anthropological Series 4. 1914.

*Mooney, James. "Myths of the Cherokee," ARBAE 19 (1900): 3–548.

Parker, Arthur C. *Parker on the Iroquois.* Syracuse, N.Y.: Syracuse University Press, 1968.

*——— *Seneca Myths and Folk Tales.* Buffalo: Buffalo Historical Society, 1923.

Rand, Silas T. *Legends of the Micmacs.* New York and London: Longmans, Green, and Co., 1894.

Savard, Rémi. *Contes indiens de la Basse Côte Nord du Saint-Laurent.* PCES 51. 1979.

Speck, Frank G. *Ethnology of the Yuchi Indians.* Anthropological Publications of the University Museum 1. Philadelphia, 1909.

———. *Naskapi: The Savage Hunters of the Labrador Peninsula,* new ed. Norman: University of Oklahoma Press, 1977.

———. *Penobscot Man.* New York: Octagon, 1976.

———. "Penobscot Tales and Religious Beliefs," JAF 48 (1935): 1–107.

†Swanton, John R. *Myths and Tales of the Southeastern Indians.* BBAE 88. 1929.

Voegelin, Charles F. *The Shawnee Female Deity.* YUPA 10. 1936.

Wallace, Paul A. W. *The White Roots of Peace.* Philadelphia: University of Pennsylvania Press, 1946.

Williams, Marianne, ed. *Kanien'kéha' Okara'shón:'a: Mohawk Stories.* New York State Museum Bulletin 427. 1976.

Wilson, Edmund. *Apologies to the Iroquois.* New York: Vintage, n.d.

Notes

Page 186/Chitimacha creator: BBAE 43, 356–58.

Pages 186–88/Natchez, Creek, and Yuchi culture myths: ibid. (Natchez); Speck 1909, 107 & 138–39 (Yuchi and Creek).

Page 188/Lucky hunter and corn mother: Mooney 1900 (Cherokee); Swanton 1929, 2 (Creek) & 9–17 (Creek) & 133 (Alabama) & 181 (Koasati).

Page 189/Corn myths: Hewitt 1918, 412 (Iroquois); Hewitt 1928, 589–90 (Iroquois); JAF 3 (1890), 214 (Wabanaki); M. L. Williams 1956, 58 (Chippewa); Dorsey 1904b, 36–37 (Arikara).

Page 190/Theft of Fire (with Rabbit): PAES 13, 46 (Yuchi). Cf. BBAE 161, 195 (Seminole); Swanton 1929, 45–46 (Creek) & 102–4 (Hichiti) & 123 (Alabama) & 203 (Koasati).

Pages 190–91/Creation myths: Mooney 1900, 239 (Cherokee); BBAE 43, 356 (Chitimacha); Speck 1909, 103–4 (Yuchi); PAES 13, 3 (Yuchi).

Pages 191–92/Female sun: Haas (Natchez, Tunica, Cherokee, Yuchi, Biloxi). See also Swanton 1929, 84; Speck 1909, 106; JAF 6 (1893), 279.

Page 192/Cherokee Orpheus myth: Mooney 1900, 252.

Page 192/*Nani Waiya:* Bushnell; Halbert. For distribution of Southeast and Northeast emergence stories, see Wheeler-Voegelin and Moore.

Page 195/Turtle island: Hewitt 1928, 482 (Iroquois); Parker 1923, 62 (Iroquois); Barbeau 1915, 292–93 (Huron); Brinton 1884, 132–34 (Delaware); Kinietz and Voegelin, 1 (Shawnee); Barnouw, 74 (Chippewa); Catlin 1973 1, 181 (Mandan); APAM 1, 61 (Gros Ventre); Mooney 1965, 225 (Arapaho).

Page 196/"People, we are still constantly hearing": M. Williams 1976, 3 & 80.

Page 196/Woman Who Fell from the Sky: Hewitt 1903 (Mohawk, Onondaga, Seneca); Hewitt 1928 (Onondaga); Parker 1923, 59 (Seneca). See also Barbeau 1915 (Huron, Wyandot); Voegelin 1936, 3–11 (Shawnee); HNAI 15, 628 (Shawnee); Flannery, 158 (Delaware); Brinton, 132 (Delaware) & 136 (New York Harbor Indians, i.e., probably Delaware, could be Mahican).

Page 197/Chief Gibson's version: Hewitt 1928.

Page 199/"Now at that time he made another": ibid., 520.

Page 201/Hungry Pleiades: Parker 1923, 83 (Seneca); JAF 13 (1900), 281 (Onondaga); Barbeau 1915, 58 (Wyandot); Mooney 1900, 258 (Cherokee); Swanton 1929, 166 (Koasati) & 242 (Natchez).

Page 202/Sky Maidens: M. L. Williams 1956, 31 (Shawnee). See also Parker 1923, 86 (Seneca); Barbeau 1915, 56 (Wyandot); Swanton 1929, 138 (Alabama); PAES 13, 231 (Yuchi).

Page 203/Thunder and Serpent: Parker 1923, 218–27; Hewitt 1918, 268 etc.; Kilpatrick and Kilpatrick, 50 & 53–56.

Page 204/Delaware and Seneca mythic trees: Parker 1968, 154.

Page 204/*Deganawida* legend: Wallace; Parker 1968, 65ff. & 101 ("white roots").

Page 206/*Glúskap* myth: Leland (Micmac, Passamaquoddy); Speck 1935 (Penobscot); Mechling (Maliseet); Rand (Micmac).

Page 206/Penobscot clan legends: Speck 1976, 216–17.

Page 207/Christianized myths from the western Wabanaki: Speck 1935 (Indians of Maine); ARBAE 43 (1938), 180–89 (Kennebec of Bécancour, Quebec); Haviland and Power, 188 (Abenaki).

Page 207/*Djokábesh* myth as told by Francois Bellefleur: Savard, 4. See also Fisher, 229–30 & 239.

Page 208/*Mésho:* Savard, 31–32. Cf. ibid., 78–79; Speck 1977, 98.

Page 209/Seneca Dark Dance: Wilson, 203–12.

Page 209/Modern Mohawk folktale: Williams 1976, 160.

Page 209/Wabanaki little people: HNAI 15, 133; Mechling, 54–55; PAES 10, 59; Speck 1935, 13; Leland.

Page 209/"Dwarflike creatures who are believed to dress and act like 'old time Indians' ": HNAI 15, 116.

Part Eight: Midwest

Bibliography

*Barnouw, Victor. *Wisconsin Chippewa Myths and Tales*. Madison: University of Wisconsin Press, 1977.

Bloomfield, Leonard. *Plains Cree Texts*. PAES 16. 1934.

———. *Menominee Texts*. PAES 12. 1928.

*———. *Sacred Stories of the Sweet Grass Cree*. National Museum of Canada, Bulletin 60, Anthropological Series 11. 1930.

Dorsey, George A. *Traditions of the Osage*. FMAS 7, no. 1. 1904. Cited as Dorsey 1904d.

Dorsey, James Owen. *The Ǫegiha Language*. Contributions to North American Ethnology 6. Washington, 1890.

———. "Osage Traditions," ARBAE 6 (1888): 373–97.

Fletcher, Alice C., and Francis La Flesche. *The Omaha Tribe*. 2 vols. Lincoln: University of Nebraska Press, 1972.

Hallowell, A. Irving. "Ojibwa Ontology, Behavior, and World View." In Dennis Tedlock and Barbara Tedlock, eds., *Teachings from the American Earth*. New York: Liveright, 1975.

Latorre, Felipe A., and Dolores L. Latorre. *The Mexican Kickapoo Indians*. Austin: University of Texas Press, 1976

Makarius, Laura. "The Crime of Manabozho," *American Anthropologist* 75 (1973): 663–75.

Michelson, Truman. *Fox Miscellany*. BBAE 114. 1937.

———. "Ritualistic Origin Myths of the Fox Indians," *Journal of the Washington Academy of Sciences* 6 (1916): 209–11.

Newcomb, William W., Jr. "The Walam Olum of the Delaware Indians in Perspective," *Texas Journal of Science* 7 (1955): 57–63.

Norman, Howard A. *Where the Chill Came From: Cree Windigo Tales and Journeys*. San Francisco: North Point Press, 1982.

———. *The Wishing Bone Cycle: Narrative Poems from the Swampy Cree Indians*. New York: Stonehill, 1976.

Radin, Paul. *The Evolution of an American Indian Prose Epic*. Special Publications of the Bollingen Foundation 3. 2 parts. 1954 and 1956.

———. *Literary Aspects of North American Mythology*. Norwood, Pa.: Norwood Editions, 1973.

———. *The Road of Life and Death*. New York: Pantheon, 1945.

———. *The Trickster*. New York: Schocken, 1972.

———. *The Winnebago Tribe*. Lincoln: University of Nebraska Press, 1970.

Skinner, Alanson. "Ethnology of the Ioway Indians." *Bulletin of the Public Museum of the City of Milwaukee* 5: 181–354. 1926.

———. "The Mascoutens or Prairie Potawatomi." Bulletin of the Public Museum of the City of Milwaukee 6:1–411. 1924.

———. *Social Life and Ceremonial Bundles of the Menomini Indians*. APAM 13, pt. 1. 1913.

*————, and John V. Satterlee. *Folklore of the Menomini Indians.* APAM 13, pt. 3. 1915.

Voegelin, Charles F., trans. *Walam Olum.* Indianapolis: Indiana Historical Society, 1954.

Whitman, William. "Origin Legends of the Oto," JAF 51 (1938): 173–205.

*Williams, Mentor L. *Schoolcraft's Indian Legends.* East Lansing: Michigan State University Press, 1956.

Notes

Page 213/Trickster-creator-deliverer: Fisher (Cree, Ojibwa, Menominee, Potawatomi, Fox, Sauk); Latorre and Latorre, 261–63 (Kickapoo); Radin 1972, 63 (Winnebago); Dorsey 1890 (gives Omaha and Ponca myths of *Mastshíngke,* mentions *Mistshinge* for Iowa and Oto).

Page 214/Animal tales still told of *Wisakedjak:* Norman 1976, 135–69; cf. Bloomfield 1930, 279–97.

Page 214/"Old agreement": Norman 1982, 17; cf. Hallowell, 150.

Page 214/*Wisakedjak* stories in Cree syllabic writing: *New York Times* 1/1/72, p. 21 ("Young Crees in Montana Educated from an Indian's Point of View").

Page 216/Rolling Head: Bloomfield 1930, 8; and Bloomfield 1934, 271.

Page 218/Red Swan: Radin 1972, 63 (Winnebago); Fisher, 249 (Cree, Fox); M. L. Williams 1956, 124 (Chippewa); Bloomfield 1928, 419 (Menominee); CNAI 19, 166 (Oto); J. O. Dorsey 1890, 219 (Omaha); G. A. Dorsey 1904d, 34 (Osage). See also PAES 14, 137 (Lakota); CNAI 3, 116–17 (Lakota); Hewitt 1928, 489 (Onondaga).

Page 219/Comparable to the *Iliad:* Radin 1954–56.

Page 219/Ojibwa treated it as a *wíndigo* story: M. L. Williams 1956, 169. On *wíndigo,* see also Barnouw; Norman 1982.

Page 219/Dying brother: Makarius, 664–65 (Menominee, Sauk, Fox, Ojibwa, Potawatomi); Fisher, 231 (Cree); Radin 1973, 11–13 & 20–21 & 22–24 & 44 & 46–47 (Winnebago); J. O. Dorsey 1890, 226–43 & 244–53 (Omaha). See also APAM 4, pt. 1, 145–47 (Assiniboin); Grinnell 1962, 149–52 (Blackfeet); Savard, 78–79 (Montagnais).

Page 220/"Gulped sobbing": PAES 1, 345.

Page 220/Sighs cause hills and ridges: ARBAE 14 (1896), 115.

Page 221/Hare "took his blanket": Radin 1972, 90.

Page 221/Chippewa Medicine Rite given to *Manabózho:* Barnouw, 43.

Page 221/Origin myth of Winnebago Rite: Radin 1970, 302. Cf. Skinner 1926, 247 (Iowa).

Page 222/Hare and Christ: Radin 1970, 328 (Winnebago); Skinner and Satterlee, 241 (Menominee).

Page 222/*Kitche Mánito* in Cree cycle: Bloomfield 1930, 18–20.

Page 222/*Walum Olum:* Voegelin 1954: Brinton 1884; Newcomb.

Page 225/Omaha clans: Fletcher and La Flesche, 134–41.

Page 225/Winnebago clans: Radin 1970, 137–38.

Page 226/*Heresgunina:* Radin 1954–56, 13 & 50–54.

Page 226/Earthmaker "created a world": Radin 1945, 253.

Page 226/Clan bundle legends and origin myths: Skinner 1913 (Menominee);

Radin 1970 (Winnebago); Skinner 1924 (Potawatomi); Michelson 1937 (Fox); Michelson 1915 (Sauk?, Kickapoo?); Skinner 1926 (Iowa); Whitman (Oto); Fletcher and La Flesche (Omaha, Osage).

Page 227/"Ho, grandmother!": Dorsey 1888, 389.

Page 228/Myth of Potawatomi Fish clan: Skinner 1924, 62.

Page 229/*Mondamin:* M. L. Williams 1956, 58.

Page 229/Osage theory of creative power: ARBAE 43 (1928), 29–30.

Page 230/Narrative of Pebble Society: Fletcher and La Flesche, 570.

Page 230/"In the beginning, Earthmaker was sitting in space": Radin 1970, 164. See also ibid., 302; Radin 1945, 17 & 252.

Page 231/"We do not believe": Dorsey 1888, 396.

Index